101 Business Tax Tips

2020/21

By

Sarah Bradford

Publisher Details

This guide is published by Tax Insider Ltd, 3 Sanderson Close, Great Sankey, Warrington WA5 3LN.

'**101 Business Tax Tips**' (formerly 101 Business Tax Secrets Revealed and 101 Tax Tips for Entrepreneurs) first published in September 2012, second edition April 2013, third edition April 2014, fourth edition September 2015, fifth edition May 2016, sixth edition April 2019 and seventh edition September 2020.

A CIP Copy of this book is available from the British Library.

ISBN 978-1-9161577-1-2

Contents

About This Guide

All businesses, large or small, like to save tax and there are many simple steps that a business can take to achieve this aim.

This guide contains 101 tax savings tips aimed at entrepreneurs. The tips follow the lifecycle of a business meaning that there is something for everyone, regardless of whether you are thinking of starting a business, a new start-up or an established business. Many of the tips apply equally to sole traders, partnerships and companies, whereas some are specific to a particular type of business.

However, it should be noted that tips in this guide are for illustration purposes only and are intended to demonstrate where tax savings can be made. The savings that can be made will depend on the precise circumstances and the examples are a guide only. Professional advice should always be sought.

Chapter 1.
Business Structure

1. Choose The Right Structure For Your Business

2. Choose Which Taxes You Pay

3. Take Advantage Of The Veil Of Incorporation

4. Save Incorporation Costs

5. Create Different Categories Of Shares In A Limited Company

6. Keep Administration Costs Low

7. Keep All Business Profits For Yourself

8. Maximise The Skill Base

9. Agree The Split Of Partnership Profits And Losses

10. Consider Purchasing An Existing Business

11. Run A Franchise

1.   Choose The Right Structure For Your Business

There are various ways in which businesses can be structured, and it is important that the structure that is chosen is the right one for the business.

There are four main options:

- sole trader;
- partnership;
- limited liability partnership; and
- limited company.

The choice of business vehicle affects the type of taxes you pay, your liability for business debts and the legal and administrative requirements imposed on the business. It will also affect the way in which business decisions are made and the sources of finance available to the business.

In deciding on the right structure for the business, it is necessary to take account of all relevant factors and also your attitude to risk.

For example, a sole trader is the simplest set-up and the proprietor gets to keep all of the profits. However, he or she is also liable for all of the business debts. The sole trader is taxed on his total income after deducting his personal allowances – the profits of the business are not taxed separately but form part of the sole trader's taxable income, together with income from other sources, such as any employment or investment income. A sole trader must also pay Class 2 and Class 4 National Insurance contributions if profits exceed the relevant trigger thresholds.

A limited company is more complicated to set up and administer, but the shareholders' liability is limited to the amount of capital that they own – a major plus. The company is taxed in its own right, and any profits that are extracted from the company will be taxed on the recipients. The tax position of the company is separate from that of the individual shareholders. The company must file annual accounts and an annual confirmation statement at Companies House. Being a director of a limited company also confers certain statutory duties.

Choose The Right Structure For Your Business

Bill wants to set up his own business. He has some money to invest but does not want to risk losing his family home if the business fails.

He is also keen to present a professional image to potential customers to help him win new business.

Having considered all the factors, Bill decides that a limited company is the right vehicle for his business. Limited liability is very important to him and he is prepared to undertake the additional administrative burden associated with a limited company in return for this.

2.   Choose Which Taxes You Pay

The choice of business vehicle will also determine which taxes are paid by your business. Sole traders and partnerships pay income tax on their profits and Class 2 and Class 4 National Insurance contributions, whereas a limited company pays corporation tax. However, there may also be income tax to pay on profits extracted from a limited company and where those profits are extracted in the form of a salary or bonus, Class 1 NICs.

The profits from a sole trader's business and a partner's share of partnership profits are taken into account in working out his or her overall income tax liability, together with income from other sources, such as any employment income, taxable interest, and dividend income. Personal allowances are available to reduce the amount on which tax is charged. To the extent that business profits exceed the proprietor's personal allowance, they are taxed at 20%, 40% or 45% for taxpayers in the UK excluding Scotland (the Scottish rates of income tax apply to Scottish taxpayers). By contrast, the taxable profits of a company are taxed at the corporation tax rate of 19% (financial years 2019 and 2020). Profits extracted from the company as salary or bonus are liable to income tax and also Class 1 National Insurance contributions. However, salary and bonus payments and the associated employer's National Insurance are deductible in computing profits chargeable to corporation tax. There is no corporation tax deduction for dividends, which must be paid out of retained profits, but in the hands of the shareholder, they are tax-free to the extent that the dividend allowance is available and otherwise at the relevant dividend rate of tax.

Gains realised by individuals are liable to capital gains tax, whereas a company pays corporation tax on chargeable gains.

All businesses with turnover of VATable goods and services above the VAT registration threshold, currently £85,000, must register for VAT. All businesses with turnover below this level can choose to register if they wish, but this is not compulsory. VAT-registered businesses with turnover above the VAT registration threshold of £85,000 must comply with the requirements of Making Tax Digital. Where the business is VAT registered but turnover is below this level, compliance with MTD for VAT is optional.

A sole trader and an individual partner in a partnership are self-employed and pay both Class 2 flat rate National Insurance contributions and Class 4 contributions on their profits if their profits exceed the relevant profit thresholds. It is the payment of Class 2 National Insurance contributions that builds up entitlement to the state pension and certain contributory benefits.

Companies do not pay National Insurance on their profits but must pay employer contributions on payments of earnings made to employees.

By choosing the structure for your business, it is also possible to choose which taxes you pay – the taxes that are paid vary depending on the structure of the business.

Choose Which Taxes You Pay

Richard wants to set up a business. Having considered the options, he decides that being a sole trader is the right decision for him.

Richard will pay income tax on any profits from his business. His income tax liability will depend on his total income from all sources.

He will pay capital gains tax on any capital gains made from the sale of business assets, etc.

He will also need to register for Class 2 National Insurance contributions and will also pay Class 4 contributions on his profits.

If his turnover exceeds the VAT registration threshold, he must also register for VAT. If his turnover is below this level, he can register voluntarily as this will allow him to recover any VAT suffered, although he must also charge VAT on any VATable supplies that he makes.

3.   Take Advantage Of The Veil Of Incorporation

Sole traders have unlimited liability for any debts that their business incurs. By contrast, a shareholder is only liable for company debts up to the amount of any share capital that they own. Limited liability is one of the main advantages of choosing to run your business as a limited company rather than as a sole trader or partnership.

A limited company is a separate legal entity from its shareholders and directors. This is known as the veil of incorporation. The shareholders' and directors' personal assets are not available to meet the debts of the company. However, the money and assets of the company belong to the company rather than to the shareholders personally.

By contrast, where an individual operates a business as a sole trader, there is no legal distinction between his or her business and private affairs. This means that the individual is personally liable for any business debts.

Take Advantage Of The Veil Of Incorporation

Jack has set up in business as a limited company. He has 100 £1 shares that are fully paid up. He is the sole shareholder.

The business collapses with debts of £10,000. Jack is not personally liable for those debts. His liability is limited to his shareholding of £100.

4.   Save Incorporation Costs

A limited company must be properly created in accordance with company law requirements and registered with Companies House. This process is known as incorporation.

Although a company formation agent, accountant, solicitor or chartered secretary can be used to incorporate the company in return for a fee, it is possible and relatively straightforward to set up the business yourself. Guidance on how to do this can be found on the Gov.uk website at www.gov.uk/limited-company-formation/register-your-company. A company can be registered online if it is limited by shares and it uses the standard article of association (also known as the 'model articles'). This service costs £12 and the company is normally registered within 24 hours. The same service can be used to register the company for corporation tax and to register for PAYE.

It is also possible to register a company by post using form IN01. The stated timescale for postal applications is 8 to 10 days and the service costs £40. A same day service is available as long as the application is at Companies House by 3 pm. This service costs £100.

However, you may wish to seek professional advice prior to setting up a company, particularly as regards to what is the appropriate share structure for your business to facilitate the tax efficient extraction of profits (see Tip 5).

Save Incorporation Costs

Bill investigates the process of setting up a company for his new business. He wants to keep costs to a minimum and uses the online incorporation service offered on the GOV.UK website. This is straightforward to use and costs him only £12.

5. Create Different Categories Of Shares In A Limited Company

One of the limitations of a limited company when it comes to setting an efficient profit extraction strategy is the need to pay dividends in proportion to shareholding; dividends are declared 'per share'. To overcome this limitation, when setting up a limited company, consider creating different classes of shares to allow the flexibility for different rights to be attributed to different shareholders. Because dividends must be paid out in accordance with shareholdings, by creating different classes of shares it is possible to declare a dividend for one class and not for another, or to declare different dividends for different classes of shares. This allows the flexibility to extract profits in a tax-efficient manner. A share structure of this nature is often referred to as an alphabet share structure, as the company can create A class shares for one shareholder, B class shares for another shareholder and so on.

Likewise, attaching different voting rights to different shares allows the decision making to be vested in one person but for another person to receive a greater share of profits.

If an alphabet share structure is not created at the outset, it is possible to create different classes of shares at a later date, as long as this is permitted by the articles of association.

When using an alphabet share structure, it is sensible to plan ahead to ensure that the shares meet the conditions for Business Asset Disposal relief (previously entrepreneurs' relief) (see Tip 100).

Create Different Categories Of Shares In A Limited Company

The Smith family are shareholders in their family company, Smith Ltd. Mr Smith holds 100 A class shares. These have full voting rights but no right to assets on a winding up.

Mrs Smith has 100 B class shares. They have no voting rights and no right to assets on a winding up.

Mr and Mrs Smith's sons, James and John, hold 50 C class shares each. They have no voting rights but have a right to a share of the assets on winding up.

Having different classes of shares allows Mr Smith to retain full control over the decision making and provides the flexibility to declare dividends for each class of share. This will enable profits to be extracted in a tax-efficient manner by tailoring dividends to utilise any unused dividend and personal allowances and basic rate bands. On a winding up, the assets would be shared equally between the children.

6.   Keep Administration Costs Low

A sole trader is the simplest business structure to set up and run. It does not have the legal requirements associated with a limited company, nor is it necessary to agree the division of profits or losses as in a partnership or to negotiate a partnership agreement. There is no incorporation process, as there is for a company, and no need to file a confirmation statement and accounts with Companies House. Consequently, the administrative burden associated with being in business as a sole trader is considerably less than for a company.

However, a person operating as sole trader must notify HMRC of their self-employment and register for National Insurance. As with all businesses, records must be kept and tax returns filed.

A sole trader is also fully liable for any business debts.

7.   Keep All Business Profits For Yourself

An individual who is in business as a sole trader gets to keep all the profits made by his or her business. By contrast, profits made by a partnership are shared between the partners in accordance with the profit sharing ratio. Any profits made by a limited company belong to the company and can be paid out to the directors/shareholders in the form of a salary, bonus or dividend (as appropriate) or retained in the company.

A sole trader is uniquely placed to enjoy all the benefits of his or her business success.

Keep All Business Profits

Lucy is in business as a sole trader. She has a successful year and makes a profit of £100,000, which is treated solely as her income.

Her sisters, Katie and Emily, are in partnership, sharing profits equally. The partnership also makes a profit of £100,000. This is due mainly to a contract negotiated by Emily. However, the profits must be shared in accordance with the profit sharing ratio and Katie and Emily each have profits of £50,000.

In each case the profits are taxed as the income of the individual concerned.

8.   Maximise The Skill Base

For a business to be successful, a range of skills are needed. Where a person operates as a sole trader, they either need to possess those necessary skills or pay an expert, such as an accountant, to provide the skills that they lack.

A partnership offers the opportunity to bring together people with different skills in a business scenario. This can strengthen the business and increase the likelihood of success. Likewise, operating as a company offers the opportunity to recruit individuals to provide the full range of skills needed. Alternatively, skills that the directors/shareholders lack can be contracted out. In a personal or family company, it may be preferable and more cost-effective to contract out payroll and IT support, for example, than to provide it in-house. External experts can provide valuable support to a business, regardless of the way in which that business is structured.

9.   Agree The Split Of Partnership Profits And Losses

The legal definition of a partnership is the relationship that subsists between persons carrying on a business in common with a view to profit.

In a simple partnership the partners share profits and losses in accordance with a pre-agreed profit sharing ratio. A partnership is not a separate legal entity and partners are jointly and severally liable for the debts and losses of the partnership.

Normally, one would want the partnership agreement to be crystal clear on the split of profits. However, where the partnership comprises a husband and wife or civil partners, it may be advantageous to have a more loosely worded agreement to provide some flexibility in profit allocation to allow profits to be split in a way that minimises their combined tax liability. This could be achieved by a clause in the agreement which provides for profits to be determined in such a ratio as is agreed by the partners.

Agree The Split Of Partnership Profits And Losses

William and Ann are husband and wife and are in partnership together. As their other income fluctuates, they decide to keep the partnership agreement loose as to the share of profits and agree the split each year depending on their other income.

In year 1 William has other income of £20,000 and Ann has no other income. The profits of the partnership are £50,000 and are allocated £35,000 (70%) to Ann and £15,000 (30%) to William to equalise income and minimise tax liabilities.

In year 2, neither has any other income and profits from the partnership are £70,000. They agree to split the profits equally.

The absence of a set profit sharing ratio in the agreement provides the flexibility to allocate profits in a tax-efficient manner.

In each case the profits are taxed as the income of the individual concerned.

10. Consider Purchasing An Existing Business

The failure rate among start-up businesses is very high. Instead of starting a new business, another option is to purchase an existing business. Although this may be more expensive initially, the success of the business is already proven, and the investment may be less risky in the long term. The aim of any business is to succeed commercially. It is also easier to attract finance for an established business than for a new start-up.

When buying an existing business, the purchaser can either buy the shares in the business (if the business is a limited company) or the assets in the business. Where the business is an unincorporated business it will be the assets that are bought.

Professional advice should be sought prior to the acquisition of an existing business to ensure that the sale is structured in a tax-efficient manner and all legal requirements are met.

11. Run A Franchise

If you fancy being your own boss but have not had much previous business experience or are unsure whether your business idea will be successful, one option worth considering is running a franchise. Under a franchise arrangement the owner of a business (the franchisor) grants a licence to another person allowing them to use the business idea in a specific geographical location. The franchisee sells the franchisor's services or products under the franchisor's established brand name and receives help and business support. The franchisee pays an initial fee to the franchisor and also a percentage of profits.

Although it can be quite expensive to buy a franchise, the business is run on a proven model with an established name and identity, and support is available from the franchisor. Banks may also be more willing to lend to a franchise than to a new start-up.

Well-known franchises include Costa Coffee, MacDonald's, Carphone Warehouse, and Subway.

Chapter 2.
Finance And Investment

12. Prepare A Business Plan

13. Choose The Right Finance Option For Your Business

14. Secure Tax Relief On Loans To A Close Company

15. Borrow Money To Buy Partnership Assets And Obtain Tax Relief For Interest

16. Beware The Return Of Funds Trap

17. Tax Relief For Business Borrowings

18. Attract Investors Under The Seed Enterprise Investment Scheme

19. Take Advantage Of The Enterprise Investment Scheme

20. Attract Investment From A Venture Capital Trust

12. Prepare A Business Plan

A new business will need money when starting up to meet the costs of equipment, premises, stock, marketing, etc. A business that does not have adequate financing will fail.

It is important to identify how much finance is required and the preparation of a business plan is an important stage in this process. A business plan is a written document that describes the business, its aims and objectives and includes financial forecasts.

Preparing a business plan is a useful exercise as it forces one to think more carefully about the business idea and whether or not it has a realistic chance of success. It can help identify potential weaknesses and also gauge success.

The business plan is fundamental to external investors and they will make the decision about whether to lend money to the business on the strength of the business plan. Banks and other financial institutions will want to see a business plan before lending money to a new business.

There are various business plan templates on the internet which are available to download for free.

13. Choose The Right Finance Option For Your Business

It is important that the financing route chosen for a business is the right route for that business. There are many different sources of finance which are appropriate for different needs.

The sources of finance available to a new business include using your own money, borrowing money from family and friends, borrowing from a bank, attracting outside investors, borrowing from other commercial lenders and securing grant finance.

Different financing options will have different tax implications and these need to be considered.

During the Coronavirus pandemic, a number of measures were introduced to provide financial support for business to help them survive. These include grants for small businesses, businesses in the retail, leisure and hospitality sectors and for Ofsted-registered nurseries, bounce-back loans, the Coronavirus Business Interruption Loan scheme and the Coronavirus Futures Fund.

It is advisable to take professional advice.

14. Secure Tax Relief On Loans To A Close Company

Tax relief is available for interest on loans where the money borrowed is used for certain qualifying purposes. Buying shares or lending money to a close company is a qualifying purpose, as long as the associated conditions are met.

A close company is one that is under the control of five or fewer participators or any number of participators if those participators are directors. Most family companies are close companies.

Relief is available for interest paid on a loan to buy ordinary shares in a close company or to lend money to a close company provided that certain conditions are met:

- you own 5% of the shares (either alone or together with associates); or

- you have some shares (not necessarily 5%) and work for the greater part of your time in the management of the company or that of an associated company.

It should be noted the availability of certain income tax reliefs is capped each year at the greater of 25% of income and £50,000. The cap applies to various reliefs, including relief for qualifying loan interest and loss relief.

Secure Tax Relief On Loans To A Close Company

XYZ Ltd is a family company. Leo owns 60% of the ordinary share capital and his wife Julia owns the remaining 40%.

Leo extends the mortgage on the family home, borrowing an additional £40,000 which he lends to the company.

As the borrowing is for a qualifying purpose, Leo is entitled to tax relief for the interest on the additional £40,000 of borrowings.

This is subject to the operation of the cap on income tax reliefs.

15. Borrow Money To Buy Partnership Assets And Obtain Tax Relief For Interest

Tax relief is available on money borrowed to buy equipment or machinery for use in a partnership, provided that the items in question qualify for capital allowances.

It may therefore be advisable to borrow money to buy equipment and machinery and to use savings for a non-qualifying purpose to maximise the tax relief available.

It should be noted that the availability of certain income tax reliefs is capped each year at the greater of £50,000 and 25% of income. Relief for qualifying loan interest is subject to the cap, which also applies to loss reliefs.

Borrow Money To Buy Partnership Assets And Obtain Tax Relief For Interest

Mo and Jake are in partnership as handymen and need to buy various tools for the partnership.

Mo has £2,000 of savings. He wants to buy the tools and also take his family on holiday but needs to borrow some money to do both.

He uses the savings to fund the holiday and takes out a £2,000 loan to buy the tools for the partnership. By using the savings to fund the holiday and the loan to fund the tools he is able to claim tax relief on the loan interest. If he had done it the other way round, he would be denied a deduction for the interest.

16. Beware The Return Of Funds Trap

As noted in Tip 14, relief is available on borrowings to fund a loan to a close company. However, relief is denied if the funds are returned to the borrower.

Beware The Return Of Funds Trap

Christopher is a director of a close company in which he owns 80% of the shares. Three years ago he lent the company £50,000, funded from his savings.

Chris now wishes to extend his home and wants his money back. He knows that he can obtain interest relief for a loan to a company but not for a loan to extend his home. He therefore borrows £50,000 and lends it to the company so that the company can repay his original £50,000.

However, he has fallen into the return of funds trap and interest relief is denied as the purpose of the loan is to return funds to him.

www.taxinsider.co.uk   101 Business Tax Tips

17. Tax Relief For Business Borrowings

Interest paid on business loans or business overdrafts is a deductible expense as long as the loan is made wholly and exclusively for the purpose of the business. The incidental costs of loan finance are also deductible. It should be noted that where the business has opted to prepare accounts using the cash basis, the deduction for loan interest and finance costs is capped at £500.

Therefore, where a business needs additional funds, borrowing those funds can be tax effective as a deduction is available for interest costs and also associated costs, such as any arrangement fee. This reduces the effective cost of the borrowings.

Tax Relief For Business Borrowings

PQR Ltd is a family company. The company wishes to expand its range of products and takes out a bank loan of £20,000 to fund the expansion. They are required to pay an arrangement fee of £500 in respect of the loan. Interest is charged at 6% per annum, giving an annual interest charge of £1,200 (£20,000 @ 6%).

The interest on the loan and the arrangement fee of £500 are deductible as an expense in computing the profits of the business. The deduction is worth £190 in respect of the arrangement fee (£500 @ 19%) and £228 in respect of the interest (£1,200 @19%). The availability of tax relief for the loan interest reduces the effective interest rate on the borrowings to 4.86% (((£1,200 - £228)/£20,000) x 100%).

26

18. Attract Investment Under The Seed Enterprise Investment Scheme

Companies can consider using the Seed Enterprise Investment Scheme (SEIS) to raise money when starting to trade. Income tax and capital gains tax reinvestment relief is available to investors in the Seed Enterprise Investment Scheme (SEIS). The aim of the SEIS is to stimulate entrepreneurship.

The company can receive up to £150,000 in SEIS investment. However, a company which has already received investment through an Enterprise Investment Scheme (see Tip 19) or from a Venture Capital Trust (see Tip 20) cannot use the SEIS to raise finance. Any finance received under the SEIS counts towards the lifetime limit of funding from venture capital schemes of £12 million (£20 million for knowledge-intensive companies).

To qualify for SEIS investment, the company must meet certain conditions, be no more than two years' old, have fewer than 25 full-time equivalent employees, and have assets of less than £200,000.

In addition, the company must:

- carry out a qualifying trade;

- be established in the UK;

- not be traded on a recognised stock exchange at the time of the share issue;

- at, the time of the share issue, have no arrangements in place to become a quoted company or the subsidiary of a quoted company;

- not control another company unless that company is a qualifying subsidiary;

- not have been controlled by another company since the date of incorporation.

Tax reliefs are available to attract investors.

Income tax relief is available to investors who subscribe for shares in a qualifying SEIS company. Shares must be held for three years. Tax relief is given at a rate of 50%. The maximum annual investment is £100,000. Relief is not available if the investor is connected with the company. Capital gains tax relief is available where gains are reinvested in qualifying SEIS shares. Relief is available for 50% of the reinvested gains. The relief is subject to the £100,000 investment cap.

Small higher risk companies that meet the requirements of the SEIS should consider using the SEIS to help them raise finance and attract investors.

Attract Investors Under The Seed Enterprise Investment Scheme

Big Ideas Ltd meets the conditions for the Seed Enterprise Investment Scheme and is keen to attract investment.

Rick sells a painting in 2020/21, realising a gain of £60,000. He makes a qualifying investment of £60,000 in Big Ideas Ltd in the same tax year. As long as all the qualifying conditions are met, one half of the gain (i.e. £30,000) is exempt from capital gains tax.

19. Take Advantage Of The Enterprise Investment Scheme

The Enterprise Investment Scheme (EIS) is one of four venture capital schemes. It is designed to help smaller higher risk companies raise finance by offering a range of tax reliefs to investors. Under the scheme it is possible to raise up to £5 million a year (up to a maximum of £12 million from venture capital funds (EIS, Seed Enterprise Investment Scheme (SEIS), Venture Capital Trusts (VCTs), and social investment tax relief (SITR)) over the company's lifetime). Companies must receive investment from a venture capital scheme within seven years of its first commercial sale.

Higher limits apply to knowledge-intensive companies.

However, where the company is newly established, before using the EIS to raise finance, consideration should be given as to whether the Seed Enterprise Investment Scheme would be more appropriate (see Tip 18).

Under the EIS, tax relief is available to individuals who subscribe for shares in an EIS company. Income tax relief is given at a rate of 30% on the cost of the shares, subject to a maximum investment of £1 million per person per year (or £2 million per person per year where the excess of £1 million is invested in knowledge-intensive companies). The shares must be fully paid up. The income tax relief is therefore worth up to £300,000 to the investor. The investor can also benefit from capital gains tax and loss reliefs.

Although an individual connected with the company cannot generally obtain income tax relief on the purchase of shares, the EIS helps companies raise finance.

A company can use the EIS scheme to raise finance if:

- it has a permanent establishment in the UK;

- it is not trading on a recognised stock exchange at the time of the share issue and does not plan to do so;

- it does not control another company (other than a qualifying subsidiary);

- it is not controlled by another company or does not have more than 50% of its shares owned by another company; and

- it does not expect to close after completing a project or series of projects.

In addition, the company and any qualifying subsidiary must not have gross assets worth more than £15 million before any shares are issued and not more than £16 million immediately afterward and have less than 250 full-time equivalent employees at the time that the shares are issued.

The company must also carry out a qualifying trade. Where the company is part of a group, the majority of the group's activities must be qualifying trades.

HMRC's Small Company Enterprise Centre can advise a company whether it meets the conditions for a qualifying EIS company.

Becoming an EIS company can help a company attract external investment.

20. Attract Investment From A Venture Capital Trust

The Venture Capital Trust (VCT) scheme was introduced to help smaller higher risk companies whose shares are not listed on a recognised stock exchange raise funds. To encourage investment, tax relief is given to investors. Income tax relief is given to investors at a rate of 30%. An investor can invest up to £200,000 a year in a VCT. Capital gains tax relief on disposal may also be available.

To attract VCT investment the company must meet certain conditions regarding its trading activities, its gross assets, its independence and its subsidiaries. The company must have no more than £15 million in gross assets, less than 250 employees and, at the time of receiving the investment, it must be less than seven years since its first commercial sale.

To qualify, a company must also:

- have a permanent establishment in the UK;

- carry out a qualifying trade;

- plan to spend the investment on a qualifying trade;

- not be listed on a recognised stock exchange at the time of the investment; and

- not be controlled by another company.

The maximum amount that can be raised is £5 million a year, subject to a lifetime limit of £12 million of investment from venture schemes. Higher limits apply to knowledge-intensive companies, which can raise up to £10 million per year and £20 million over their lifetime.

Companies that meet these requirements could consider tapping into VCT funding. Companies interested in raising investment from a venture capital scheme can seek advanced assurance that an investment would meet the conditions of the scheme. This can be beneficial in attracting investors.

Chapter 3.
Early Years

1. Register With HMRC And Avoid Penalties

2. Choose Your Accounting Date

3. Choose Your Corporation Tax Payment Date

4. Consider Whether To Register For VAT Voluntarily

5. Cash Basis v Accruals Basis

6. Save Work By Joining The VAT Flat Rate Scheme

7. Limited Cost Business and the VAT Flat Rate Scheme

8. Carry Back Early Year Losses

9. Choose The Method Of Relief For Early Year Losses

10. Extend The Loss To Capital Gains

11. Consider Not Claiming Capital Allowances

12. Claim Relief For Pre-Trading Expenditure

13. Claim Relief For Capital Expenditure Incurred Before The Start Of Trading

21. Register With HMRC And Avoid Penalties

Regardless of whether you are running your business as a sole trader, a company or a partnership, you need to tell HMRC.

If you are a sole trader, you must register as self-employed for self-assessment and for National Insurance. This should be done by 5 October in the business's second tax year. HMRC may charge a penalty for a failure to register by this date. This is to allow the tax return for the first year of the business, due by 31 January after the end of the tax year, to be filed online.

An individual can register as self-employed online. This can be done online by following on the GOV.UK website at www.gov.uk/log-in-file-self-assessment-tax-return/register-if-youre-self-employed. HMRC will set up records from the information provided. Where a person is a partner in a partnership, they will also need to register for self-assessment. To do this, they will need the partnership's ten-digit unique tax reference. This can be done online: see www.gov.uk/log-in-file-self-assessment-tax-return/register-if-youre-a-partner-or-partnership. The partner who is the nominated partner for the partnership must register the partnership for tax.

If you run your business through a limited company, after you have registered your company with Companies House, you must register for corporation tax. This must be done within three months of starting to do business. You can register online (see www.gov.uk/limited-company-formation/set-up-your-companyfor-corporation-tax). To register, you will need your unique tax reference (UTR). This is a ten-digit number which is sent to you automatically once you have registered your company with Companies House. Any business where turnover exceeds the VAT registration threshold will also need to register for VAT (see Tip 24).

Failure to notify may trigger late notification penalties, or for VAT a late registration penalty.

Register With HMRC And Avoid Penalties

DEF Ltd was dormant for some years following incorporation. The company becomes active and makes a taxable profit for the year to 31 March 2020 on which corporation tax of £4,000 is due. The company has not notified HMRC that it is active, nor has it told HMRC that it is liable to pay corporation tax or delivered a return within 12 months of the end of the accounting period.

A penalty is charged on the potential lost revenue of £4,000.

A late payment penalty will also be charged on corporation tax paid late.

By notifying on time, this could have been avoided.

101 Business Tax Tips

22. Choose Your Accounting Date

For the self-employed, the choice of accounting date can be crucial as it will determine which profits are taxed twice and also the level of overlap relief available on cessation or a change of accounting date.

To make life easier, you may wish to choose an accounting date of either 31 March or 5 April to coincide with the tax year. This will eliminate any overlap profit.

However, if you choose a date other than 31 March or 5 April, some profits will be taxed twice in the early years. These 'overlap' profits are carried forward until either the business changes its year end or ceases, when relief is given in the form of overlap relief.

A date early in the tax year (e.g. 30 April) will give the greatest lag between the end of the accounting period and the date on which the tax must be paid.

Choose Your Accounting Date

Holly starts in business as a sole trader on 1 January 2020. For 2019/20, she is assessed on actual profits from 1 January 2020 to 5 April 2020.

The profits on which she is assessed in the second year depend on her choice of accounting date.

If she chooses an accounting date of 31 March, in 2020/21 she is taxed on the profits for the year to 31 March 2021. Only profits from 1 to 5 April 2020 are taxed twice.

36

However, if she chooses an accounting date of 31 December, in 2020/21 she will be taxed on the profit for the year to 31 December 2020. The profits for the period from 1 January 2020 to 5 April 2020 were also taxed in 2019/20. These will be taxed twice as overlap profits.

Relief for overlap profits is given either when the business ceases or on a change of accounting date.

23. Choose Your Corporation Tax Payment Date

Corporation tax is generally payable nine months and one day after the end of the accounting period. By choosing your accounting date you also choose the date by which your corporation tax is due. Where a business is seasonal this provides the flexibility to choose a payment date where the company is relatively cash rich.

Choose Your Corporation Tax Payment Date

Zak provides gardening services through his company ZK Gardens. He is very busy during the summer months and quiet during the winter. By choosing a year end of say, 31 October, his corporation tax will be due on 1 August, when his cash flow is good.

By contrast, if he chooses a year end of 31 March, his corporation tax will be due on 1 January, which falls during his quiet time when his cash flow is less healthy.

Choosing a 30 April accounting date would mean that his corporation tax will be due on 1 February. As this coincides with the self-assessment due date for his personal tax of 31 January, a different date may be preferable from a cashflow perspective.

24. Consider Whether To Register For VAT Voluntarily

A business must register for VAT if the VATable turnover in the previous 12 months is more than the VAT registration threshold (set at £85,000 until 31 March 2022) or it is expected that this threshold will be exceeded within the next 30 days. A business whose turnover is below this level does not have to register for VAT but may choose to register voluntarily. This will allow VAT suffered on purchases and expenses to be reclaimed. This may offset the burden of charging VAT and accounting for it to HMRC.

Where a company is registered for VAT and has turnover in excess of the VAT registration threshold, it must comply with the requirements of Making Tax Digital for. If the business has turnover below the VAT registration threshold and has chosen to register for VAT voluntarily, they can choose whether to enter MTD for VAT or not. However, if a business starts to comply with the requirements voluntarily, they can leave the MTD service at a later date, as long as their turnover is still below the VAT registration threshold, and revert to submitting VAT without using MTD-compatible software. Under MTD for VAT, a business must keep digital records and file VAT returns using MTD-compatible software.

Consider Whether To Register For VAT Voluntarily

Simon has turnover of £30,000 a year. He does not need to register for VAT but chooses to do so. As a result, he is able to recover his input VAT. In the first year of VAT registration, he recovers input tax of £3,500, making voluntary registration worthwhile.

25. Cash Basis v Accruals Basis

The accruals basis is the default basis of accounts preparation for traders. However, unincorporated traders who meet the eligibility tests can instead elect to prepare accounts under the cash basis.

Under the accruals basis (also known as the 'earnings basis'), income and expenditure are matched to the period to which they relate rather than being taken into account when the income is received or the expenditure paid. This means that it is necessary to take account of debtors and creditors and work out prepayments and accruals. Relief for capital expenditure is given in the form of capital allowance. The accruals basis is the default basis for traders in the absence of a cash basis election.

Under the cash basis, income is taken into account when it is received, and expenditure is taken into account when it is paid. There is no need to match income and expenditure to the period to which it relates. Where the cash basis is used, relief for capital expenditure is given as a deduction from profits unless the expenditure is of a type for which a deduction is specifically prohibited (see Tip 53).

The cash basis is only an option for eligible traders. To qualify for the cash basis, the trader must have cash basis receipts of not more than £150,000. Once in the cash basis, a trader can remain in it as long as cash basis receipts are not more than £300,000. These limits are doubled for universal credit claimants. Traders wishing to use the cash basis must elect in their self-assessment tax return for it to apply. The cash basis can only be used by unincorporated business. Partnerships qualify as long as they comprise wholly of individuals; LLPs cannot use the cash basis.

Eligible traders should consider using the cash basis to simplify the calculation of their taxable profits. The cash basis also provides automatic relief for bad debts as income is not recognised until payment is received.

Cash Basis v Accruals Basis

John is a sole trader and prepares accounts to 5 April each year. On 31 March 2020 he invoices a customer £180 for work done on 28 March 2020. The customer pays the bill on 10 April 2020. John ordered some parts for £300 on 21 March 2020, receiving an invoice dated that day. He paid the invoice on 18 April 2020.

Under the accruals basis, the invoice issued to the customer of 31 March 2020 would be taken into account in the year to 5 April 2020, as would goods purchased on 21 March 2020. However, under the cash basis, the income would not be taken into account until 2020/21, as it was received in that year. Likewise, the expenditure on the parts would be taken into account in 2020/21 rather than 2019/20, as the payment date fell in 2020/21.

26. Save Work By Joining The VAT Flat Rate Scheme

Smaller VAT-registered businesses can save a significant amount of work by joining the flat rate scheme. The scheme can be used by businesses that have taxable turnover of less than £150,000. Under the scheme, the VAT payable over to HMRC is calculated as a percentage of VAT-inclusive turnover. The percentage depends on the nature of the business (see www.gov.uk/vat-flat-rate-scheme/how-much-you-pay).

A discount of 1% on the flat rate percentage is given to businesses in their first year of VAT registration, saving them money.

Once a business has joined the scheme, it can remain in it even if turnover exceeds £150,000 in a year as long as total income, including VAT, is not more than £230,000 in a year.

Using the flat rate scheme removes the need to record separately the VAT charged on purchases, reducing the time spent doing the books. However, VAT must still be charged on sales within the scope of VAT and a VAT invoice issued on which VAT is shown separately.

However, if you are a limited cost business, the scheme may not be beneficial for you (See Tip 26).

Save Work By Joining The VAT Flat Rate Scheme

Betty starts up in business as a photographer. She registers for VAT and joins the flat rate scheme. She is not a limited cost business (see Tip 26).

In year 1, her VAT-inclusive turnover is £24,400. The appropriate flat rate percentage is 11% but as she is in her first year of registration, she receives a discount of 1%. She must pay over VAT of £2,440 (£24,440 @ 10%) a quarter to HMRC.

In year 2, her VAT-inclusive turnover has increased to £26,000 a quarter. She no longer benefits from the discount and pays VAT over to HMRC of £2,860 (£26,000 @ 11%) over to HMRC.

27. Limited Cost Businesses And The VAT Flat Rate Scheme

Businesses that are classed as 'limited cost businesses' have a higher flat rate percentage than for their business type. The VAT flat rate percentage for a limited cost business is 16.5%.

A business is a limited cost business if the amount that it spends on 'relevant goods' is either:

- less than 2% of the VAT flat rate turnover; or

- greater than 2% of the VAT flat rate turnover but less than £1,000 per year (£250 per quarter).

The VAT flat rate turnover is the turnover of the business inclusive of VAT.

Only 'relevant goods' are taken into account in applying the turnover test to determine if a business is a limited costs business. Relevant goods are goods used exclusively for the purposes of the business, but excluding:

- vehicle costs including fuel (unless the business is one operating in the transport sector using a vehicle that it owns or leases);

- food or drink for the proprietor or staff;

- capital expenditure on goods of any value;

- goods for resale, leasing, letting or hiring out where that is not the business's main business activity;

- goods for resale or to hire out, unless this is the business's main activity;

- goods forming promotional items, gifts or donations.

In VAT Notice 733, HMRC provide the following examples of relevant goods include:

- stationery and office supplies;

- gas and electricity used exclusively for the business;

- fuel for a taxi owned by a taxi firm;

- stock for a shop;

- cleaning products to be used exclusively for the business;

- hair products used to provide hairdressing services;

- standard software;

- food to be used for meals for customers;

- goods provided by a subcontractor and itemised separately;

- goods brought without VAT being charged if not otherwise excluded.

HMRC also provide the following examples of goods that are not relevant goods:

- accountancy fees;

- advertising fees;

- items leased or hired to the business;

- goods not used exclusively for a business (such as the electricity to supply a home and an office located in a home);

www.taxinsider.co.uk   101 Business Tax Tips

- fuel for a car unless the business operates in the transport sector;

- electronic devices, such as laptops or mobile phones for use in the business (as these constitute capital expenditure);

- anything provided electronically, such as a downloaded magazine (as this is regarded as a service);

- software that is download;

- bespoke software, even if not provided electronically;

- stamps and postage costs; and

- goods bought solely to meet the turnover test to prevent the business from being classed as a limited costs business if the quantity of goods is such that they cannot reasonably be used by the business.

Where a business is a limited costs business, they pay VAT to HMRC at the rate of 16.5% of VAT inclusive turnover. This is equivalent to 19.8% of net (VAT exclusive) turnover.

Thus, a limited cost business pays virtually all the VAT they charge over to HMRC, with virtually no allowance for VAT incurred. Where the VAT incurred on items that are not relevant goods is significant, the business may be much worse off staying in the flat rate scheme.

Such businesses should evaluate whether the additional administration costs incurred as a result of coming out of the flat rate scheme and working out VAT in the normal way is justified in relation to the VAT saved.

Limited Costs Businesses And The VAT Flat Rate Scheme

Joe operates a consultancy business and is VAT registered. His turnover is £25,000 plus VAT (i.e. £30,000 inclusive of VAT).

His expenditure on relevant goods is £400 plus VAT. However, he also incurs expenditure of £7,000 plus VAT on non-relevant goods.

The VAT on the relevant goods is £80 (20% of £400) and the VAT on the non-relevant items is £1,400 (20% of £7,000).

Joe would meet the test for a limited cost trader and under the VAT flat rate scheme would pay VAT of £4,950 over to HMRC.

However, if Joe came out of the flat rate scheme, he would only pay VAT of £3,520 (£5,000 – (£80 + £1400). Joe is much better off outside the VAT flat rate scheme, as he is able to recover the VAT on non-relevant items, such as services.

28. Carry Back Early Year Losses

A business often makes losses in the early years of the trade. There is a special loss relief available to individuals (whether sole traders or partners in a partnership), which allows a loss made in the tax year in which the individual first carried on the trade or in any of the three succeeding years, to be relieved against total income of the preceding three tax years. The loss is relieved against an earlier year before a later year.

Carrying back the loss relieves the loss at the earliest opportunity and generates a tax repayment.

It should be noted relief for certain losses is capped each year at the greater of 25% of income and £50,000.

The cap applies to various types of loss relief and to relief for qualifying interest. In some cases, the operation of the cap may limit the amount of early years' loss relief that can be obtained.

Further, if the cash basis is used, it is not possible to relieve losses sideways or to carry them back.

See also Tip 28 for alternative ways to relieve a loss in the early years of a business.

Carry Back Early Year Losses

Jessica starts her business in 2020/21, making a loss in the first year of £15,000.

In 2017/18, she had total income of £70,000. In 2018/19 and 2019/20, she had income of £80,000 and £65,000 respectively.

Carrying the loss of £15,000 back three years and setting it against her total income for 2017/18 of £70,000 will reduce her income for that year to £55,000 (£70,000 - £15,000) and generate a tax repayment of £6,000 (£15,000 @ 40%) plus interest.

29. Choose The Method Of Relief For Early Year Losses

As noted in Tip 28, losses made in the opening years of a business can be carried back against the total income of the preceding three tax years.

However, this is not the only option for relieving early year losses. The loss can also be set against other income for the year in which the loss was incurred or the previous tax year or carried forward against future trading profits.

The basic aim of loss relief planning is to obtain relief at the highest marginal rate of tax and earlier rather than later. The decision as to which route to take to relieve the loss will depend on the level of other income, expected future profits, income of previous years and the rates of tax in the years concerned. Care should also be taken to preserve personal allowances.

It should be noted that relief for losses and qualifying loan interest is subject to a cap, which is set at the greater of £50,000 and 25% of income.

Where the loss arises in a trade carried on by an individual or a partner in a non-active capacity, claims for sideways loss relief (setting off the loss against general income of same or preceding year) are capped at £25,000 a year.

Choose The Method Of Tax Relief For Early Year Losses

Jane starts her business on 1 January 2019 and makes a loss of £10,000 for 2019/20.

She has other income of £30,000 in 2019/20 and had income of £8,000 in 2018/19. In 2016/17 and 2017/18 she had income of £5,000 and £6,000 respectively.

She secured a major contract in May 2020 and as a result expects her profits to be £100,000 in 2020/21.

Jane can relieve the loss against her other income of 2019/20 of £30,000, but she will only receive relief at the basic rate of 20%. However, if she carries the loss forward and sets it against the profits of £100,000 for 2020/21, she will receive relief at 40%. By choosing this option, utilising the loss saves her tax of £4,000, rather than the £2,000 that she would have saved if she had set it against other income of 2019/20.

It is not worthwhile carrying the loss back to 2016/17 as her income for that year is offset by her personal allowances and carrying the loss back would be a waste.

30. Extend The Loss To Capital Gains

If relief for a trading loss is claimed against other income for the current or previous tax year, the claim can be extended by election to capital gains tax if there is insufficient income in the year to fully utilise the loss.

This can be useful in some circumstances.

This relief allows an unused loss to be set against the chargeable gains for the year, reducing the capital gains tax payable for the year. However, the loss is set against gains before utilising the annual exemption and consequently a claim will not always be worthwhile. In this situation it is better to carry the loss forward against future trading profits than set it against any capital gains.

Extend The Loss To Capital Gains

Paul makes a loss in 2020/21 of £25,000.

He has no other income in that year, but makes a capital gain of £80,000 from the sale of shares.

He elects to extend the loss to capital gains. The loss is set against the capital gain of £80,000 saving him capital gains tax of £5,000 (£25,000 @ 20%).

As his remaining gains (£55,000, being the £80,000 gain less loss relief of £25,000) exceed the capital gains tax annual exempt amount of £12,300 for 2020/21, setting the loss against capital gains does not waste this exemption.

Setting the loss against the capital gain provides immediate relief for the gain.

However, if Paul expects to make significant profits in future years, he may be able to obtain relief for the loss at a rate of 40% if he is a higher rate taxpayer by carrying the loss forward to set against future profits from the same trade. The loss would then be worth £10,000, rather than the £5,000 relief obtained by setting it against his capital gain.

Paul will need to evaluate the benefit of relief now at a lower rate against the possibility of relief in the future at a higher rate in deciding how best to use the loss.

31. Consider Not Claiming Capital Allowances

Capital allowances augment a loss. In certain circumstances it may be better not to claim the allowances as this may preserve personal allowances. This strategy will allow higher allowances to be claimed in later years when profits are higher.

Note: where the trader has elected to compute profits using the cash basis, claims for capital allowances are not in point (with exception of cars when simplified expenses are not used). Instead, capital expenditure is relieved under the cash basis capital expenditure rules.

Consider Not Claiming Capital Allowances

Polly makes a loss of £18,000 in the second year of her business. She prepares accounts using the accruals basis. The loss includes capital allowances of £8,000. She has other income of £22,000 in the same year (2020/21).

By not claiming capital allowances, the loss is reduced to £10,000. She can set this against her other income without wasting her personal allowance (£12,500 for 2020/21)). The loss of £10,000 is set against her other income of £22,000, reducing it to £12,000, which is covered by her personal allowance for 2020/21, leaving her with £500 of her personal allowance unused.

Had she claimed capital allowances, she would have wasted £8,500 (£12,500 - £4,000) of her personal allowance as all but £4,000 of her other income (£22,000 - £18,000) would have been covered by the loss.

By not claiming the capital allowances now, higher allowances will be available in future years when profits may be higher.

If Polly is married or in a civil partnership and her partner pays tax at the basic rate, she could consider using the marriage allowance to transfer 10% of her personal allowance (£1,250 for 2020/21) to her partner, reducing per personal allowance to £11,250. She could then claim capital allowance of £750 to reduce her income from £12,000 to £11,250 to exactly match her reduced personal allowance.

The ability to tailor a capital allowances claim allows the individual to optimise their tax position.

32. Claim Relief For Pre-Trading Expenditure

It is likely that expenses will be incurred in setting up a business prior to the commencement of that business. The opportunity to claim relief for pre-trading expenditure should not be overlooked.

For income tax purposes, relief is available for pre-trading expenditure if:

- it was incurred within seven years of the start of the actual trade;

- had the expenditure been incurred after the commencement of the trade, it would have been allowed as a deduction; and

- it is not otherwise deductible in computing profits.

In deciding whether the expenditure would have been allowed as a deduction had it been incurred once trading commenced, normal rules apply – the business must satisfy the 'wholly and exclusively' rule (see Tip 34).

The pre-trading expenditure is treated as incurred on the first day of trading. Consequently, it is taken into account in computing the profits of the first accounting period.

Relief is similarly given for corporation tax purposes.

It should be noted that different rules apply to capital expenditure incurred before the start of the trade (see Tip 33) and also for reclaiming VAT on pre-registration supplies.

Claim Relief For Pre-Trading Expenditure

Benny starts trading as a sole trader on 1 October 202. In preparation for the start of his business he incurs various expenditures that would have been deductible had they been incurred after trading commenced.

The pre-trading expenditure amounts to £2,750. This is treated as incurred on 1 October (the first day of trade) and deducted in computing his profits for 2020/21.

33. Claim Relief For Capital Expenditure Incurred Before The Start Of Trading

Relief for pre-trading expenditure (see Tip 32) does not extend to capital expenditure. However, similar rules allow capital expenditure to be treated as having been incurred on the first day on which trading begins.

The way in which relief for pre-trading capital expenditure is given will depend on whether the trader prepares accounts under the accruals basis or whether an election has been made to use the cash basis.

Under the accruals basis, capital allowances may be claimed and any expenditure qualifying for capital allowances is treated as if it had been incurred on the first day of trading. However, eligibility for first-year allowances and the annual investment allowance are determined by reference to the date on which the expenditure was actually incurred.

Where the trader has opted to use the cash basis (see Tip 25), relief for pre-trading capital expenditure is given as a deduction in computing profits, unless the capital expenditure is of a type for which a deduction is specifically disallowed (as is the case for land and cars). The deductible expenditure is treated as if it were incurred on the first day of trading. Capital allowances can be claimed under the cash basis in respect of cars, but only if simplified expenses (see Tip 37) are not being used to claim a deduction in respect of business expenses for that vehicle.

Claim Relief For Capital Expenditure Incurred Before The Start Of Trading

David starts trading on 1 September as a sole trader. He prepares accounts on the accruals basis. In preparation for trading, he spends £80,000 on plant and machinery in February 2020. Due to the Covid-19 pandemic, the launch of his business was delayed. The expenditure qualifies for the annual investment allowance and David receives a deduction of £80,000 against his 2020/21 profits. For capital allowance purposes, he is treated as having incurred the expenditure on 1 September.

Lucy also starts trading on 1 September. However, she elects to prepare accounts using the cash basis. In February 2020, she spends £10,000 on shelving. She is able to claim a deduction in computing the profits for 2020/21 as if she had incurred the expenditure on 1 September.

Chapter 4:
Deductions For Business Expenses

34. Claim A Deduction For All Allowable Business Expenses

Significant amounts of tax can be saved by ensuring that you claim a deduction for all allowable business expenses. Generally, these are expenses which are incurred in the course of earning profits for the business.

The general rule is that business expenses can be deducted when calculating taxable profit as long as they are incurred wholly and exclusively for the purposes of the business. This means that private expenses cannot be deducted from business profits (but see Tip 35 for dual-purposes expenditure).

This test is less stringent than the corresponding test for deductibility of employees' expenses, which also requires that the expense was necessarily incurred. There is no requirement that it was necessary to incur a business expense for it to be deductible, only that it was incurred wholly and exclusively for business purposes.

Where accounts are prepared using the accruals basis, a deduction is not given for capital expenditure, for which capital allowances are given instead (see Chapter 5).

Where the trader has elected to use the cash basis (see Tip 25), relief for capital expenditure is given in accordance with the cash basis capital expenditure rules (see Tip 53). These allow capital expenditure to be deducted when computing profits unless the capital expenditure is of a type for which such a deduction is specifically disallowed (as is the case for land and cars).

To ensure that deductible expenses are not overlooked, it is important that good records are kept, together with invoices and receipts.

Claim A Deduction For All Allowable Business Expenses

Judd has a small business, which he runs as a sole trader. For the year in question, he incurs business expenses of a revenue nature of £12,000. The expenses are incurred wholly and exclusively for the purposes of his business.

The business expenses are deducted from turnover in the calculation of his taxable profits.

Had he omitted to deduct the expenses he would have paid unnecessary tax. This would have cost him £2,400 (£12,000 @ 20%) if he is a basic rate taxpayer and £4,800 (£12,000 @ 40%) if he is a higher rate taxpayer. It is important that records are kept of all business expenses.

35. Claim A Deduction For The Business Element Of Dual-Purpose Expenses

Although you cannot claim a deduction for private expenditure when computing business profits, if costs are incurred for both business and private purposes, you can claim a deduction for the business proportion where this can be separately identified. This situation may arise where a person uses his or her car, computer or mobile phone for both business and private purposes.

The costs must be apportioned between the business and private elements on a just and reasonable basis. For example, an itemised phone bill could be used to identify business and private calls and a mileage log could be maintained to identify the split between business and private travel in a car used for both purposes.

> ### Claim a Deduction For The Business Element Of Dual-Purpose Expenses
>
> Mark is a sole trader. He has a mobile phone that he uses both for business and private calls. He prepares accounts to 31 March each year.
>
> In the year to 31 March 2021, his mobile phone bills came to £1,200. He works out that 90% of his calls are for business and the remaining 10% are personal.
>
> Mark is able to claim a deduction of £1,080 (£1,200 @ 90%) when computing the taxable profit of his business.

36. Don't Overlook Common Expenses

Although all businesses are different and the expenses incurred will vary depending on the nature of the business, it is important to make sure that you don't overlook any expenses for which a deduction could be claimed.

Common business expenses include:

- accountancy costs;

- advertising;

- motor expenses;

- travel expenses;

- insurance;

- stationery and postage;

- power and water;

- rent;

- staff costs;

- bank charges;

- telephone costs;

- internet charges;

- cost of goods for resale;

- packaging costs.

37. Use Mileage Rates To Save Work

If you are a sole trader or in partnership and you use a car, motorcycle or goods vehicle for the purposes of your trade, you can claim a deduction for the costs incurred in doing so. To save work and remove the need to keep detailed records of actual costs incurred, under the simplified expenses rules a statutory deduction can be claimed by reference to a fixed rate per mile. Simplified expenses can be used regardless of whether the trader prepares accounts using the cash basis or the accruals basis (see Tip 25).

For 2020/21, the appropriate mileage rate for cars and vans is 45p per mile for the first 10,000 business miles and 25p per mile thereafter. The appropriate mileage rate for motorcycles is 24p per mile.

The mileage rate covers the cost of buying and maintaining the vehicle, and also depreciation. Consequently, where mileage rates are used, it is not possible to claim a further deduction for fuel costs, servicing and MOT and such like. However, a further deduction can be claimed in respect of incidental costs incurred in connection with a particular journey, such as road tolls or the congestion charge. A deduction can also be claimed for the finance element where the vehicle is acquired under a hire purchase arrangement or finance lease.

However, it is not possible to claim a deduction by reference to mileage rates if capital allowances have ever been claimed in respect of the vehicle.

If the business has elected to prepare accounts under the cash basis, it can claim a deduction by reference to mileage rates as long as capital allowances have not been claimed. However, a business using the cash basis cannot claim a deduction by reference to mileage rates for goods vehicles and motorcycles if a deduction has been claimed for the cost of acquiring them in computing the taxable profits of the business under the cash basis capital expenditure rules.

You do not have to use the mileage rates for all vehicles. However, once you have chosen to use this method for a particular vehicle, you must continue to use this method as long as you use the vehicle for your business.

Use Mileage Rates To Save Work

Sarah is a sole trader. She uses her own car for business and private journeys. In the year to 31 March 2021, she undertook 14,000 business miles.

To save work, she claims a deduction based on the appropriate mileage rate of £5,500 when computing her taxable profits for the year to 31 March 2021.

The deduction is computed as follows:

10,000 miles@ 45p per mile = £4,500

4,000 miles @ 25p per mile = £1,000

Total deduction   = £5,500

38. Use Actual Costs Rather Than Fixed Rates

Although using fixed rates to calculate deductions saves a lot of work, if the costs actually incurred exceed the fixed rate costs it is beneficial to calculate the deduction by reference to the actual costs. However, on the downside this will mean that records of actual costs will need to be kept. It is a question of balancing the additional work against the additional deduction that may be available.

Where mileage rates are not used to calculate the deduction in respect of a car, capital allowances may be available in respect of expenditure on the car.

Use Actual Costs Rather Than Fixed Rates

Polly has a top of the range sports car which she uses for business purposes. She keeps a record of actual mileage and servicing costs for a year.

She undertakes 10,000 business miles and her actual costs are £6,000. If she claimed a fixed rate deduction by reference to mileage rates (see Tip 35) she would be entitled to a deduction of £4,500 (10,000 miles @ 45p per mile).

By basing the deduction on actual costs, she is able to enjoy a higher deduction, reducing profit and saving tax. The additional deduction of £1,500 saves tax of £600 assuming Polly is a higher rate taxpayer.

She can also claim capital allowances in respect of the capital expenditure on the car.

39. Home Office: Deduction For Business Use (Fixed Costs)

Many small businesses are run from home and a proportion of the costs associated with running and maintaining a home can be deducted in computing the profits of the business.

The fixed costs associated with a home are incurred regardless of whether there is any business use of the property. These include rent, mortgage interest, insurance, council tax and general repairs.

Where a part of the house is set aside specifically for business use, a proportion of the fixed costs can be deducted in computing business profits. The apportionment should be made on a just and reasonable basis, such as by reference to floor area or the number of rooms.

However, where part of the home is used exclusively for business use, that part will not benefit from the capital gains tax main residence exemption if the property is sold and any gain apportioned to the business part will be taxable. However, in practice this is rarely a problem as any taxable gain on the business part is usually covered by the capital gains tax annual exemption.

Home Office: Deduction For Business Use (Fixed Costs)

Evie runs a small business from home. She uses one room exclusively for the purposes of her business. Her home has ten rooms.

For the year in question she pays home insurance of £300, rent of £12,000 and council tax of £1,500; a total of £13,800. She claims a deduction of 10%, i.e. £1,380, in computing her business profits.

40. Home Office: Deduction For Running Costs

The costs associated with a home include fixed costs (see Tip 39) and running costs. Running costs vary with use.

Where a business is run from home, a deduction is available for the additional running costs incurred as a result. This will include additional electricity, water, gas, cleaning, etc.

If it is not possible to identify the additional amount incurred as a result of business use, the total bill will need to be apportioned between business and private use. The basis of apportionment should be reasonable. An apportionment based on hours worked or number of people may give a more accurate result than using floor area or the number of rooms.

See Tip 41 for claiming the alternative statutory deduction rather than a deduction based on actual costs.

Home Office: Deduction For Running Costs

Phil runs a business from the family home. The annual electricity bill is £2,000 and Phil determines that based on the hours worked, his business use accounts for 60% of the bill. He claims a deduction of £1,200.

41. Business Use Of Home: Fixed Deduction

Under the simplified expenses rules, a statutory deduction is available for business use of home. The statutory deduction can be used by sole traders and by partnerships. It is not available to companies. Consider using simplified expenses to claim a fixed rate reduction to save the work that is involved in working out a deduction based on actual costs.

You can claim a fixed deduction each month in respect of business use of your home. The amount of the deduction depends on the number of hours spent at home during that month working wholly and exclusively on the business (including any hours worked by employees). The fixed monthly deductions are as shown in the table below.

No. of hours worked at home in month	Monthly deduction
25 to 50	£10
51 to 100	£18
101 or more	£26

Business Use Of Home: Fixed Deduction

Nicola is self-employed as a beautician. She carries out treatments both at clients' houses and at home. She also undertakes the business administration at home. Each month she spends 60 hours working at home. She claims a fixed rate deduction by reference to the set amount of £18 per month.

This equates to an annual deduction of £216.

42. Business Premises Used As A Home: Statutory Disallowance

In the situation where a trader lives in premises that are also the business premises (as may be the case, for example, for someone running a bed-and-breakfast or a boutique hotel), a deduction can be made for premises cost that relate to the business when working out the profits for the business. However, the costs relating to the private living accommodation must be disallowed.

To simplify matters, a fixed rate disallowance can be claimed where a trade is carried out at premises which are used mainly for the purposes of that trade but which are also used as the person's home. Rather than having to work out the actual apportionment for home and business use, the private use disallowance is determined by relevant to the number of people living in the premises. The private element is deducted from the actual total expenses to arrive at the allowable business deduction. The use of this fixed rate disallowance is available to sole traders and to partnerships.

The disallowance for the non-business element depends on the number of people who occupy the premises as a home (or otherwise than for the purpose of the business) and is computed on a monthly basis. The monthly disallowance for non-business use is as set out in the table below.

Number of occupants	Non-business element
1	£350
2	£500
3 or more	£650

To obtain the best possible deduction, the outcomes obtained by using apportioned actual costs (Tips 39 and 40) should be compared to that obtained by reference to the statutory disallowance for private use. While using the fixed disallowance may save work, if the deduction calculated by reference to actual costs is higher, this will save more tax.

Business Premises Used As A Home: Statutory Deduction

Elliott runs a bed and breakfast and lives on the premises with his wife. He runs the business as a sole trader.

In a particular month in 2020/21, he incurs premises' expenses of £2,000.

He claims a deduction for premises' expenses by reference to the alternative statutory basis.

The non-business element for two occupants is £500 per month. The business element is therefore £1,500 (£2,000 - £500) and he claims a deduction of £1,500 for the month in question.

43. Deduction For Uniform Or Protective Clothes

As a general rule a deduction is not given for everyday clothes, even if these are only worn for business purposes. The wholly and exclusively test is not met as the clothes also provide warmth and decency. This rule means that, for example, a trader is not allowed a deduction for the costs of a normal business suit or shirts.

However, a deduction is given for the cost of a uniform or protective clothes. A uniform may just be normal clothes which feature the business logo. By swapping your work suit, shirt and tie for ones featuring the business logo, the costs become deductible. The logo will have the added benefit of promoting the business.

Deduction For Uniform Or Protective Clothes

Jason is a self-employed personal trainer. He invests in personalised training kit featuring his business logo. By swapping his general sports gear for sports clothing featuring his business logo he is able to claim a deduction for his clothing costs.

44. Deduct Allowable Travel Expenses

Most businesses incur travel expenses and these can be significant. It is therefore important that you deduct allowable travel expenses when computing your profits.

The rules relating to travel expenses can be complicated, so consider taking advice to ensure you claim what you can and don't fall foul of the rules.

In the case of a sole trader or partnership, if the business is based away from home, the costs of travelling to the business base from home are not deductible. The costs of commuting are not allowable as these are incurred to put the person in a position to work rather than being incurred in running the business. However, if the business is based at home the costs of travel from home to the premises of a customer or supplier are deductible.

Where the proprietor or partner uses his or her own car or van for work, the deduction may be based on a mileage rate (see Tip 37). If public transport is used, the deduction is the actual cost incurred. There is no requirement to take the cheapest mode of transport – so you can travel first class to a business meeting and claim the full deduction.

Where the business is run as a company, all travel costs met by the company are deductible in computing the company's profits. However, if the company meets the costs of private travel of an employee or director (such as home-to-work travel costs) this may give rise to a benefit in kind tax charge on the recipient and a Class 1A NIC liability on the company.

It should be noted that tax relief is not given for home-to-work travel where a worker's services are provided to an engager through an employment intermediary (such as a personal service company or an umbrella company) and the worker is subject to the direction, supervision or control of the engager.

Deduct Allowable Travel Expenses

David runs a small business as a sole trader from a unit on a nearby business estate.

He drives to work each day. The costs of this journey cannot be deducted as an expense of the business.

He has regular meetings with suppliers. He drives from the office to the station and takes a train to the meeting, returning by train and car back to the office at the end of the day. The associated travel costs are deductible in computing the taxable profits of his business.

45. Claim A Deduction For Training Costs

A self-employed person may be able to claim a deduction for training costs.

However, a distinction is drawn between training to update existing skills and training to acquire a new skill. The former is treated as revenue expenditure and is deductible in computing the profits of the business, whereas the latter is regarded as capital expenditure which is not deductible as an expense.

Many professions require their members to undergo regular training to keep their skills up to date. These costs can be deducted in computing the profits, along with any associated travelling costs.

Claim A Deduction For Training Costs

Dermot is self-employed as a dentist. He attends a training course on the latest techniques. The course costs £2,000 and as the expenditure is treated as revenue rather than capital, it is deductible in computing his business profits.

46. Allowable Entertaining Costs

As a general rule entertaining expenses are not deductible. However, there are some types of expenditure for which a deduction is allowed.

The main exception is entertaining of employees, the costs of which can be deducted. However, depending on the nature of the entertaining, this may give rise to a benefit in kind taxable on the employee.

Promotional events are not treated as entertainment and the costs can be deducted. However, the cost of any food, drink or any other hospitality is not allowable.

Allowable Entertaining Costs

LMN Ltd is a family company.

The company holds a Christmas party each year, which is attended by staff and their partners.

The company can deduct the costs of holding the party in computing its business profits. This disallowance for entertaining does not apply to staff entertaining.

As long as the cost is less than £150 per head, the employees will not suffer a benefit in kind tax charge as the benefit will fall within the exemption for Christmas parties and similar functions.

47. Deduction For Business Gifts

Although business gifts are not deductible as a general rule, there is an exception for small gifts that carry a conspicuous advertisement for the trader, such as a branded diary, mouse mat or pen. However, for a deduction to be forthcoming the gift must not be food, drink or tobacco and the cost of all gifts to the recipient in the tax year is capped at £50.

A deduction can also be claimed for the cost of free samples given to the public.

Deduction For Business Gifts

Roger is a self-employed gardener. He wants to give his customers a gift at Christmas. By giving them a diary featuring the logo of his business, he is able to claim a deduction for the cost of the gifts.

Had the diaries not been branded, the deduction would not have been allowed.

48. Obtain Relief For Bad Debts

Where the accruals basis is used, a deduction can be made for a bad or doubtful debt in the year in which the debt becomes bad or doubtful, or a later year. This may be of particular relevance to 2020/21 due to the impact of the Covid-19 pandemic.

It is important to keep track of bad debts and to claim relief for any that become bad. If this is not done the trader may end up paying tax on income that has not actually been received.

Where the cash basis is used, relief is given automatically for bad debts, as income is not recognised until it is received; consequently, where a bill is not paid, it is not taken into account as taxable income of the business. Therefore, under the cash basis, there is no need to claim relief for bad debts.

If accounts are prepared on the accruals basis, there is no automatic relief. The income is recognised in the period in which the work is undertaken, regardless of whether the invoice has been paid. However, a deduction can be claimed when preparing the accounts for debts that are genuinely bad. Likewise, a provision can be made for doubtful debts.

Obtain Relief For Bad Debts

Josef is a builder. He carries out a job for a customer and invoices the customer £750. Josef prepares his accounts under the accruals basis and this invoice is included in his turnover.

The customer fails to pay the bill and Josef eventually discovers that the customer has been declared bankrupt.

Josef writes off the debt and claims a deduction of £750.

Jan is also a builder, but he elects to prepare his accounts under the cash basis. He invoices a customer £200 for a repair, but the customer moves away without paying the bill. As the income is never received, it is not taken into account in computing Jan's profits. As he uses the cash basis, the relief for the bad debt is given automatically.

49. Deduct The Cost Of Professional Subscriptions

Most professions require members to pay an annual subscription to a professional association for the right to use the qualification and designatory letters.

Where the taxpayer is self-employed, a deduction can be made in computing business profits for the cost of the professional subscription where the profits from that profession are assessed on the member. Subscriptions to local professional societies or branches are also deductible if the object of the branch or society is mainly professional.

Where the subscriptions are paid by a company, they are deductible in computing the profits of the company. As long as the subscription is on HMRC's list (List 3), the employee will not suffer a benefit in kind tax charge.

Deduct The Cost Of Professional Subscriptions

Dinesh is a self-employed accountant. He is a member of the ICAEW and pays an annual membership fee of £700. He deducts this when computing the profits of his profession.

50. Deduct Incidental Costs Of Loan Finance

Many businesses need to secure finance at some point in their lifecycle, whether to fund the initial start-up or in order to grow the business. During the Covid-19 pandemic, many businesses may have needed to take out loans in order to survive. These may be in the form of bounce back loans or loans made under the Coronavirus Business Interruption Loan Scheme.

The incidental costs of acquiring finance can be deducted in computing the profits of the business and should be claimed. Costs which may be allowable include:

• legal and professional expenses associated with negotiating the loan and preparing the documents;

• underwriting commissions, brokerage and introduction fees;

• land registry fees;

• search fees;

• valuer's fees;

• commitment fees for making a loan available; and

• commission(s) for guaranteeing a loan.

However, it should be noted that where profits are computed on the cash basis, there is a general prohibition on the deduction of interest, apart from a £500 allowance. However, the £500 maximum applies both to the deduction of interest and any incidental costs of loan finance, capping the total deduction at £500.

Deduct Incidental Costs Of Loan Finance

Hamish takes out a bank loan to fund the expansion of the business. He incurs professional fees of £500 in connection with the loan and pays an arrangement fee of £200. Hamish prepares accounts under the accruals basis.

He is able to deduct £700 in respect of these expenses when computing his business profits.

Had Hamish elected to prepare accounts under the cash basis, the total deduction for interest and the associated incidental costs of obtaining the finance would be capped at £500.

51. Insure The Key Person

The success of the business may rest on one individual and insurance (key man insurance) may be taken out to protect against loss of profits resulting from the death, critical illness, accident or injury of that person. This may provide peace of mind.

As an added benefit, the premiums on such a policy are allowable in calculating the profits of a company or a partnership (but not a sole trader) if the sole purpose of taking out the insurance is to meet a loss of trading income arising from the loss of services of a key person, rather than protecting against a capital loss.

Insure The Key Person

Jack and Jill are directors and shareholders in the family company. Jack is responsible for generating the business and Jill undertakes the administration work.

The company takes out a key man insurance policy to protect against loss of profits should Jack be unable to work due to illness or death. The premiums are an allowable deduction.

However, had the policy been taken out to protect the value of the shares, the premiums would not be allowable.

52. Don't Be Tempted To Deduct Personal Items

There is something of a myth that if you have your own business you can 'put' expenses through the business (and if the business is VAT registered, reclaim the input tax). This is very dangerous. Not only does it create extra work as these items need to be disallowed in the accounts, further, if they are left in as deductions, it may trigger enquiries into the accounts and possibly a tax investigation.

Only expenses that relate wholly and exclusively to the business are allowable as a deduction against profits. Under no circumstances should private expenditure be treated as a business expense. The temptation to put private expenses through the business should be resisted at all costs. However, see Tip 35 for items used for both business and private purposes.

The same applies for VAT. Under no circumstances should VAT on personal items be reclaimed.

Don't Be Tempted To Deduct Personal Items

Malcolm wants to undertake some DIY projects at home. He buys some materials and tools, which cost £480 plus VAT – a total cost of £576. He decides to 'put it through the business', claiming a deduction for the net cost of £480 when computing his business profits and reclaiming the associated VAT of £96 when completing his VAT return.

This is picked up in a compliance check by HMRC and Malcolm suffers penalties and interest on underpaid tax as a result.

Business and personal expenditure should always be kept separate.

Chapter 5.
Deductions For Capital Expenditure

53. Deduct Capital Expenditure Under Cash Basis

54. Obtain Relief For Capital Expenditure Under The Accruals Basis Via Capital Allowances

55. Capital Allowances Must Be Claimed

56. Obtain Immediate Relief for Capital Expenditure

57. Take Advantage Of The Temporary Increase In The AIA

58. Beware Chargeable Accounting Periods Spanning 31 December 2020

59. Claim WDAs Instead Of AIA

60. Tailor Your Claim

61. Capital Allowances And Losses

62. Time Your Capital Expenditure To Accelerate Relief

63. Claim Capital Allowances For Mixed-Use Assets

64. Buy A Green Car And Claim FYAs

65. Choose Lower Emission Cars For Higher Capital Allowances

66. De-Pool Short Life Assets

67. Write Off Small Pools

53. Deduct Capital Expenditure Under Cash Basis

Where the cash basis applies, relief for capital expenditure is, in the main, given as a deduction in computing profits, rather than via the capital allowances system.

A deduction for capital expenditure is permitted under the cash basis rules unless the expenditure is of a type for which a deduction is specifically disallowed.

The limited disallowance covers capital expenditure on:

- an item of a capital nature incurred on, or in connection with, the acquisition or disposal of a business or a part of a business; and

- an item of a capital nature incurred on, or in connection with, education or training.

- It also prohibits a deduction for expenditure on an item of a capital nature incurred on, or in connection with, the provision, alteration or disposal of:

- any asset that is not a depreciating asset (broadly, one with a useful life of more than 20 years);

- any asset that is not acquired or created for use on a continuing basis in the trade;

- a car;

- land;

- a non-qualifying intangible asset; or

- a financial asset.

However, while expenditure on a car cannot be deducted from profits, capital allowances can be claimed – but only if the simplified expenses system (see Tip 37) is not used.

The ability to deduct capital expenditure under the cash basis provides immediate relief for that expenditure in the period in which it is incurred. On the flip side, capital receipts are taken into account in computing profits where a deduction was given for the corresponding capital expenditure.

Deduct Capital Expenditure Under Cash Basis

Tony is a self-employed handyman. He uses a range of small tools in his job, which he replaces periodically. He opts to prepare his accounts using the cash basis. He prepares accounts to 31 March each year.

In the year to 31 March 2021, he spends £3,200 on new tools, the cost of which he deducts in computing his profits for that year.

54. Obtain Relief For Capital Expenditure Under The Accruals Basis Via Capital Allowances

The way in which relief is given for capital expenditure depends on whether accounts are being prepared under the cash basis or under the accruals basis. Where a cash basis election is made, relief for capital expenditure is given as a deduction in computing profits, unless the expenditure is of a type for which such a deduction is specifically disallowed (see Tip 53 for deducting capital expenditure under the cash basis).

Where taxable profit is computed under the accruals basis, expenditure on capital items cannot be deducted as an expense when computing taxable profits. Instead, relief for capital expenditure is given in the form of capital allowances. Plant and machinery capital allowances are available for a wide range of business assets, including cars, vans, computers, tools, machinery, equipment and furniture used in the business.

To claim capital allowances, the asset must be used wholly or partly for the purposes of the business and you must expect it to last at least two years.

There are different types of capital allowances. The AIA provides immediate relief for most types of plant and machinery capital allowances (with the exception of cars), writing down allowances provide relief over a longer period, at the rate of 18% or 6% depending on the type of asset. Some assets, such as new low-emission cars, are eligible for 100% first-year allowance (see Tip 64).

All businesses that prepare accounts using the accruals basis are likely to have some capital expenditure that will qualify for capital allowances and the chance to obtain relief should not be overlooked.

55. Capital Allowances Must Be Claimed

Capital allowances are not given automatically. They must be claimed, and they must be claimed within the time limit.

A claim can be made in the tax return. This will be the self-assessment return for an individual, the partnership return for a partnership or the corporation tax return for a company.

The time limit by which capital allowances must be claimed depends on the nature of the business:

- Self-employed: 12 months after the 31 January deadline for filing the return.

- Partnership: 12 months after the 31 January deadline for filing the return.

- Company: 12 months after the filing date for the return for the accounting period to which the claim relates.

Capital Allowances Must Be Claimed

Elizabeth is a self-employed caterer. She prepares accounts to 31 March and purchases various items of catering equipment during the year to 31 March 2021 in respect of which capital allowances are claimed.

She claims the allowances in her 2020/21 tax return, which is filed by the filing deadline of 31 January 2022.

The deadline for claiming capital allowances for 2020/21 is 31 January 2023. This is 12 months from the filing date for the 2020/21 return of 31 January 2022.

56. Obtain Immediate Relief For Capital Expenditure

Businesses can claim immediate relief for capital expenditure on most items of plant and machinery by means of the annual investment allowance (AIA). Capital expenditure up to the AIA limit qualifies for a 100% deduction against profits. The permanent level of the AIA is set at £200,000, but it is temporarily increased to £1 million for the two-year period from 1 January 2019 to 31 December 2020 (see Tip 57). Transitional rules apply to periods that span 1 January 2019 and 31 December 2020 (see Tip 58).

Once the AIA has been used up relief is given by means of the writing down allowance. The AIA is not compulsory. Writing down allowances can be claimed instead (see Tip 59).

The AIA cannot be claimed in respect of cars. However, a first-year allowance is available in respect of low emission cars (see Tip 64).

Obtain Immediate Relief For Capital Expenditure

Luca spends £5,000 on computers, printers and other office equipment for his business. He claims the AIA and obtains immediate relief for his expenditure.

57. Take Advantage Of The Temporary Increase In The AIA

The annual investment allowance (AIA) is temporarily increased to £1 million for the period from 1 January 2019 to 31 December 2020. The allowance will revert to its permanent level of £200,000 from 1 January 2021.

Where a chargeable accounting period falls wholly within the period from 1 January 2019 to 31 December 2020, the AIA is £1 million (proportionately reduced where the chargeable period is less than 12 months). Where the period spans 1 January 2019 or 31 December 2020, transitional rules apply (see Tip 58).

Where larger capital projects are on the agenda, consider timing the expenditure to take advantage of the temporary increase in the AIA and achieve relief for expenditure sooner.

Take Advantage Of A Temporary Increase In The AIA

K Ltd is planning ahead for investment in new equipment costing £800,000. The company prepares accounts to 31 December each year.

If the company incurs the expenditure in the year to 31 December 2020, assuming that the AIA is not otherwise utilised, they will be able to claim the AIA in respect of the full amount of the expenditure, obtaining relief against profits in the year in which the expenditure is incurred. However, if the investment is delayed until the year ending 31 December 2021, they will only be able to claim the AIA in respect of £200,000 of the expenditure and would need to claim writing down allowance for the remaining £600,000; losing some the immediate corporation tax savings that the AIA provides.

58. Beware Chargeable Accounting Periods Spanning 31 December 2020

As noted in Tip 58, the annual investment allowance (AIA) is temporarily increased to £1 million for two years from 1 January 2019. However, transitional rules apply where the chargeable accounting period spans 1 January 2019 or 31 December 2020. The transitional rules can catch the unwary, particularly where the period spans 31 December 2020.

The AIA limit reverts to £200,000 from 1 January 2021. Where the chargeable period spans 31 December 2020, the chargeable period is split into two parts – the period up to and including 31 December 2020 and the period from 1 January 2021 onwards.

The AIA for periods spanning 31 December 2020 is the sum of:

1. the AIA entitlement for up to an including 31 December 2020 based on the cap of £1 million applying to that period; and

2. the AIA entitlement for the period on or after 1 January 2021 based on the cap of £200,000 applying to that period.

However, a further cap equal to the AIA entitlement for the period on or after 1 January 2021 applies to expenditure incurred on or after that date (rather than capping it at £200,000 as is the case for pre 1 January 2019 expenditure under the transitional rules that applied where the chargeable period spanned 1 January 2019). This can seriously restrict the available AIA.

Take Beware Chargeable Accounting Periods Spanning 31 December 2020

L Ltd is planning is planning to invest £750,000 in new equipment in the next two years. They prepare accounts to 31 January.

For the year to 31 January 2021, the transitional rules apply in working out the AIA limit as the period spans 31 December 2020.

The AIA for the period is £933,333 ((11/12 x £1 million) + (1/12 x £200,000). However, a further cap of £16,667 applies to any expenditure incurred on or after 1 January 2021 (this is the AIA for the period 1/1/21 to 31/1/21, being 1/12 x £200,000).

Therefore, as long as the company incurs the expenditure in the period 1/2/20 to 31/12/20, they can claim the AIA for the full amount as the qualifying expenditure is less than the AIA limit for the period. However, if they incur the expenditure in January 2021, they will only be able to claim the AIA for £16,667 of the expenditure, claiming WDAs for the balance of £733,333. This will delay the relief for the expenditure and increase the corporation tax bill for the year to 31 January 2021.

Timing is key.

59. Claim WDAs Instead Of AIA

Although the annual investment allowance (AIA) gives immediate relief for capital expenditure, there may be circumstances when it is preferable to spread relief for the expenditure over several years and claim the writing down allowance (WDA) instead.

The WDA is an annual allowance that writes off unrelieved capital expenditure. Capital expenditure is generally allocated to one of two pools – a main rate pool and a special rate pool. The current rate of WDA is 18% for the main pool and 6% for the special rate pool.

The WDA is applied to the total of the written down value of the pool brought forward plus any capital expenditure in the period allocated to the pool, less any disposal proceeds.

It will be worthwhile claiming WDAs rather than the AIA if profits are low and claiming the AIA would create a loss which may not be relieved for some time. It may also be preferable to claim WDAs rather than the AIA if the asset is likely to be sold in the not too distant future, triggering balancing charges.

Claim WDAs Instead Of AIA

Harry is a sole trader. He prepares accounts to 31 March.

In May 2020 he incurs capital expenditure of £50,000 on plant and machinery. This is the only capital expenditure in the year to 31 March 2021. The written down value brought forward on the main pool is £20,000. Prior to deduction of capital allowances, his profits are £30,000. He has no other income.

Although the expenditure is within the AIA limit for the year to 31 March 2020 and Harry could claim the AIA in full, this would turn the profit into a loss and he would waste his personal allowance for the year. Instead he claims a WDA for the year of £12,600 (18% of £70,000 being WDV b/f of £20,000 plus additional expenditure in year of £50,000), preserving his personal allowance and spreading relief for the capital expenditure over a number of years.

60. Tailor Your Claim

You can tailor your capital allowances claim to suit your circumstances. It is not a case of claiming either the AIA or WDA, nor is it necessary to use up any remaining AIA before claiming WDAs on the balance. Further, there is generally no requirement to claim capital allowances at all.

By mixing the claims, you can claim the allowances that give the best tax result.

Tailor Your Claim

Adam is a sole trader.

In the year to 31 March 2021 he incurs capital expenditure of £20,000. He has unrelieved expenditure brought forward of £5,000. His profit before the deduction of capital allowances is £26,000.

He claims an annual investment allowance of £13,500, reducing his profit to £12,500.

The remaining £6,500 of capital expenditure is allocated to the general pool. He could claim a writing down allowances of £2,070 (18% (£5,000 + £6,500)), but chooses instead not to claim a WDA for this year as doing so would waste some of his personal allowance.

After claiming an AIA of £13,500, the profit for the year is reduced to £12,500 (£26,000 - £13,500), which is offset exactly by Adam's personal allowance for 2020/21 of £12,500. Tailoring the claim allows Adam to preserve his full personal allowance for the year.

61. Capital Allowances And Losses

Capital allowances can create or augment a loss.

If the loss is fully relievable without losing personal allowances, it may be worthwhile claiming allowances as this will save tax.

However, if claiming capital allowances will waste personal allowances it may be preferable not to claim them to reduce the loss and preserve allowances.

If the loss can only be relieved by carry forward against future profits, once again it may be preferable not to claim capital allowances as this will provide more flexibility going forward.

Capital Allowances And Losses

Joel has a loss for the year to 31 March 2021 before taking account of capital allowances of £6,000. This is a loss for the 2020/21 tax year.

He has incurred capital expenditure in the year of £10,000.

He has no other income.

In the previous tax year (2019/20) he had income of £18,500.

He does not make a claim for the annual investment allowance (AIA). Instead, the capital expenditure is added to the pool, so that WDAs can be claimed in a later year.

He carries the loss back against the income of the previous year, reducing his income for that year to £12,500 and retaining his personal allowance for 2019/20 of £12,500.

Had he claimed capital allowances (either AIA or WDA) he would have increased the loss carried back and wasted part of his personal allowance for 2020/21.

62. Time Your Capital Expenditure To Accelerate Relief

The timing of your capital expenditure around the year end will determine when relief is given and, where the AIA limit is exceeded, how relief is given. Bringing forward expenditure a few days around the year end will bring the relief forward 12 months.

However, in the unlikely event that the AIA allowance has already been used up, it may be better to wait until the start of the new year so that you can claim the AIA for that year, rather than claiming the WDA.

Where the chargeable period spans 31 December 2020, the impact of the transitional rules should be taken into account (see Tip 58). Also, the timing of the expenditure should, where relevant, seek to make best use of the temporary increase in the AIA to £1 million for the two years to 31 December 2020 (see Tip 57).

Time Your Capital Expenditure To Accelerate Relief

James is a sole trader. He prepares accounts to 31 March.

He is investing in new computer equipment for his business. The equipment costs £10,000. If he incurs the expenditure on 2 April 2021 (which falls in the year to 31 March 2022), he will receive relief in 2021/22.

By accelerating it a few days to 28 March 2021 (which falls in the year to 31 March 2021, he will receive the relief in 2020/21.

Accelerating the expenditure by a few days brings the relief forward by one year.

63. Claim Capital Allowances For Mixed-Use Assets

The fact that an asset is used both for business and private purposes does not mean that capital allowances are denied. Some relief can be claimed to reflect the business use of the asset. However, the personal element must be disallowed. For sole traders and partners where an asset is used for both business and private purposes, it is given its own pool to enable the disallowance in respect of the private use element to be calculated.

Where there is any business use of an asset, capital allowances can be claimed in respect of the business use.

Claim Capital Allowances For Mixed-Use Assets

Greg is a sole trader. He buys a new car for £20,000, which he uses for both business and private purposes. The car has CO_2 emissions of 90g/km and as such it qualifies for the writing down allowance at the rate of 18%.

The expenditure is incurred in the year to 31 March 2021.

The car is used 70% for business purposes and 30% for private use.

The WDA is £3,600 (£20,000 @ 18%).

This is reduced by 30% (£1,080) to reflect the private use.

Greg is therefore entitled to allowances of £2,520 for 2020/21 in respect of the car.

64. Buy A Green Car And Claim FYAs

Cars do not qualify for the annual investment allowance. However, it is possible to obtain full relief for expenditure on a car in the year of purchase if you buy a new low emission car that qualifies for a first year allowance (FYA) of 100%.

If the expenditure is incurred between 1 April 2018 and 31 March 2021, the FYA is available for cars with CO_2 emissions of up to 50g/km. Expenditure on cars with CO_2 emissions in excess of 50g/km do not qualify for a FYA, only the writing down allowance (see Tip 62). If the emissions are more than 110g/km, WDAs are given at the special rate of 6%.

It should be noted that FYAs are only available for new and unused low emission cars that meet the emission criteria – second-hand cars do not qualify, even if the emissions are less than 50g/km.

Buy A Green Car And Claim FYAs

Gabby is a sole trader and prepares accounts to 31 March each year.

She wishes to buy a new car which she will use solely for business purposes. She buys a car in August 2020.

She chooses one with CO_2 emissions of 40g/km. The car costs £18,000.

As the car is a new car and the CO_2 emissions are less than 50g/km she can claim the FYA and write off the full cost of the car against her profits of the year to 31 March 2021.

65. Choose Lower Emission Cars For Higher Capital Allowances

Cars that do not qualify for first year allowances (see Tip 64) or in respect of which the FYA is not claimed, are instead given a writing down allowance (WDA). The rate of WDA depends on whether the car is allocated to the main rate pool or the special rate pool, which in turn depends on its level of CO_2 emissions.

Where the expenditure is incurred on or after 1 April 2018, expenditure on cars is allocated to the main rate pool if the car's CO_2 emissions are 110g/km or less. Cars with CO_2 emissions above 110g/km are allocated to the special rate pool. As noted in Tip 64 a FYA may be claimed in respect of new cars with very low emissions (50g/km or less from 1 April 2018 to 31 March 2021).

Assets in the main rate pool attract a WDA of 18%, whereas those in the special rate pool attract a WDA of 6% (. By choosing a car with emissions below the 110g/km threshold, a higher WDA is available, reducing taxable profits and saving tax in the short term.

Choose Lower Emission Cars
For Higher Capital Allowances

Brad is looking into buying a new car for his business. He is a sole trader.

The car he likes costs £20,000 and he is deciding between two different models, one with CO_2 emissions of 95g/km and one with CO_2 emissions of 135g/km. He plans to buy the car in September 2020.

If he chooses the car with emissions of 95g/km he will receive a WDA of 18%. However, if he chooses a car with CO_2 emissions of 135g/km, he will receive a WDA of 6%. In the first year, choosing the lower emission car will mean that Brad can claim a WDA of £3,600, as opposed to a WDA of £1,200 if he chooses the car with higher emissions.

Assuming Brad is a higher rate taxpayer, choosing the lower emission car will save him £960 ((£3,600 - £1,200) @ 40%) in tax for that year. He will receive relief for his expenditure on the car over a shorter time period if he chooses the lower emission car.

66. De-Pool Short Life Assets

Special rules apply to short life assets. If the expected useful life of the asset is no more than eight years from the end of the chargeable period in which the expenditure was incurred, an election can be made to treat the asset as a short life asset.

Where such an election is made, the asset is given its own pool. Writing down allowances are given at the main pool rate of 18%. When the asset is sold, balancing allowances or charges are determined by reference to the written down value of the single asset pool. If the asset has not been disposed of by the eighth anniversary of the end of the chargeable period in which it was acquired, the written down value of the single asset pool is transferred to the main rate pool. A short life election could be considered if the AIA has been used up or to prevent a large balancing charge on disposal.

De-Pool Short Life Assets

Jessica has purchased new computer equipment for her business, which cost £2,000. She expects to keep the computer for three years. She does not wish to claim the AIA. She makes a short life asset election.

After two years the written down value on the pool is £1,345. The following year she sells the computer equipment for £800.

By making a short life asset election she is entitled to a balancing allowance of £545 (£1,345 less the sale proceeds of £800) on disposal.

Without the election, the disposal proceeds would have been swallowed up by the main rate pool. Had the AIA been claimed, a balancing charge of £800 would have arisen on the sale.

67. Write Off Small Pools

Once the balance on the main rate or special rate pool drops below £1,000, you can write off the whole balance by claiming the small pools allowance. This saves the need to make on-going claims for small allowances and also accelerates the relief.

Write Off Small Pools

Craig runs a small business. At the start of the chargeable period, the written down value on the main pool is £950As this is less than £1,000, he can claim the small pools allowance and write off the remaining balance of £950. He therefore obtains immediate relief for the pool balance.

Had he not claimed the small pools allowance, he would have been entitled to a WDA of £171.

Chapter 6.
Extracting Profits From A Family Company

68. Pay A Small Salary To Preserve State Pension Entitlement

Entitlement to the state pension and contributory benefits is contingent on having paid or been credited with sufficient National Insurance contributions. A person needs 35 qualifying years in order to secure entitlement to the full single-tier state pension. Fortunately, it is possible to achieve this for zero cost.

Persons with earnings between the lower earnings limit (£120 per week for 2020/21) and the primary earnings threshold (£183 per week for 2020/21) are treated as paying NICs at a zero rate. These notional contributions preserve entitlement to the state pension and contributory benefits.

For 2020/21 the primary and secondary thresholds are not aligned. The secondary threshold is set at £169 per week and the primary threshold is set at £189 per week.

For 2020/21, setting the salary between £120 per week and £183 per week will ensure that the year is a qualifying year for state pension purposes for zero NIC cost to the employee. This equates to an annual salary of between £6,136 and £8,632. As this is below the personal allowance, providing the person does not have a second job to which the personal allowance has been allocated or other income utilising the allowance, no PAYE tax should be due either.

However, where the director/employee is aged 21 or over, secondary contributions will be payable at 13.8% on earnings above £169 per week, unless the employment allowance is available. This is equivalent to £8,788 a year.

See Tip 69 for the optimal salary where the employment allowance is not available and Tip 70 for the impact of the employment allowance on the optimal salary level.

Under real time information (RTI), details of the amount paid to the employee must be reported to HMRC electronically. HMRC's free Basic PAYE Tools software package can be used for this purpose.

Pay A Small Salary To Preserve State Pension Entitlement

Ian and Caroline are directors of their family company. To preserve entitlement to the state pension and contributory benefits they decide to pay themselves a salary of £7,000).

As this is between the lower earnings limit (£120 per week for

2020/21) and the primary earnings threshold (£183 per week for 2020/21) they get the benefit of notional National Insurance contributions but do not have to pay any actual employee contributions. As it is also below the secondary threshold of £169 per week for 2020/21, no employer contributions are payable either.

However, under RTI they need to make a submission to HMRC each time that they make a payment. They can use HMRC's free software package, Basic PAYE Tools, for this purpose.

While paying a salary at this level is sufficient to ensure that the year is a qualifying year for state pension purposes, from a tax perspective, it may be worth paying a higher salary– see Tips 69 and 70 for details.

69. Optimal Salary Where EA Not Available

A common profit extraction strategy is to pay a salary up to the 'optimal' level and to extract further profits as dividends. The optimal salary is the maximum salary that can be paid before it becomes more efficient from a tax and National Insurance perspective to extract further profits as dividends. The level of the optimal salary will depend on the primary and secondary thresholds for National Insurance purposes, the level of the personal allowance and, where the director is aged 21 or over, whether the employment allowance (EA) is available.

As the (EA) is not available for companies where the sole employee is also a director, it is not a consideration for most personal companies. It may, however, be available in a family company set up.

Where the employment allowance is not available, it is possible for 2020/21 to pay a salary equal to the secondary threshold of £8,788 without paying any National Insurance (employee's or employer's) or, assuming that the personal allowance (set at £12,500 for 2020/21) is not used up elsewhere, any personal tax.

However, while secondary National Insurance at 13.8% is payable on a salary in excess of £8,788, increasing the salary to align with the personal allowance of £9,500 is beneficial. This is because both salary payments and employer's National Insurance are deductible for corporation tax and for 2020/21 at 19% the corporation tax rate is higher than the rate of employer's National Insurance at 13.8%. The effect of this is that the corporation tax deduction outweighs the small amount of employer's National Insurance payable.

Once the primary threshold of £9,500 is reached, any further payments attract employee's National Insurance at 12%, as well as employer's National Insurance at 13.8%. The combined National Insurance hit at 25.8%

is higher than the associated corporation tax deduction of 19%. Consequently, once the salary level reaches £9,500 it is more efficient to extract further profits as dividends.

Thus, the optimal salary level for 2020/21 where the EA is not available and the director is 21 or over is £9,500 a year (£189 per week, £792 per month).

Some secondary National Insurance contributions will need to be paid over to HMRC. However, if a salary of £792 per month is paid and an annual earnings period is used, it will only be necessary to pay the NIC over to HMRC in the final month of the year. If a director wishes to avoid the administration associated with this, they could instead pay a slightly lower salary of £8,788, equal to the secondary National Insurance threshold for 2020/21.

70. Optimal Salary Where The EA Is Available

Employers are able to claim an employment allowance (EA) of up to £4,000 a year for 2020/21 which reduces the amount of employer's Class 1 NIC that they pay. However, the allowance is not available to companies where the sole employee is also a director. This is the case for many personal service companies (but see Tip 69 on the optimal salary where the EA is not available and Tip 71 on preserving entitlement to the EA).

Where the employment allowance is available and not fully utilised against secondary NI contributions payable in respect of other employees' earnings, it is beneficial to pay a salary equal to the personal allowance (set at £12,500 for 2020/21) than on equal to the primary threshold of £9,500.

As the availability of the EA means that no employer's National Insurance is due, on salary payments above £9,500 until the personal allowance is used up, only employee's National Insurance at 12% is due. Because salary payments are deductible for corporation tax purposes, any additional salary paid saves corporation tax at 19%. The corporation tax saving (at 19%) will outweigh the primary NI contributions (at 12%) on any salary paid in excess of the primary threshold (set at £183 per week for 2020/21).

Assuming the personal allowance is not otherwise utilised, no income tax is payable on the salary until the personal allowance (£12,500 for 2020/21) is reached. Once the salary reaches the level of the personal allowance, any further salary will attract income tax at 20%. The combined tax and employee's National Insurance hit at 32% outweighs the associated corporation tax relief at 19%. Once the salary reaches the level of the personal allowance, it is more efficient to extract further profits as dividends.

Consequently, where the employment allowance remains available (and assuming the personal allowance is not utilised elsewhere), the optimal salary for 2020/21 is one equal to the personal allowance of £12,500.

It should be noted, however, where the employee is not a director, he or she must be paid at least the National Living Wage (if aged 25 or over), set at £8.72 per hour from 1 April 2020, or the National Minimum Wage if the employee is under the age of 25.

If the employee/director is under 21 or an apprentice under the age of 25, no employer's NIC is payable for 2020/21 until the employee's earnings exceed £962 per week. See Tip 72 for the impact that this has on the optimal salary calculation.

Claim The EA To Pay A Higher Salary

Susan is the director in her family company. She is 35. For 2020/21 she pays herself a salary equal to her personal of £12,500. Her husband John is also employed in the company.

In the absence of the NIC Employment Allowance she would pay employer NIC of £512.26 = ((£12,500 - £8,7888) @ 13.8%).

However, as the company has at least one other employee and the employment allowance is available, the employer's NIC would be offset by the NIC employment allowance of £4,000, such that no actual employer's NIC is payable.

However, Susan will still pay employee's NIC on the part of the salary in excess of the primary threshold (£9,500 for 2020/21) at the rate of 12%. This equates to £360 ((£12,500 - £8,632) @ 12%). As her salary is covered by the personal allowance of £12,500 for 2020/21, she will not pay any income tax on it.

Salary payments are deductible for corporation tax purposes. A salary of £12,500 will generate a corporation tax deduction of £2,375 (£12,500 @ 19%), compared to a corporation tax deduction of £1,805 on a salary equal to the primary threshold of £9,500 (£9,500 @ 19%); an additional corporation tax saving of £570 (£2,375 - £1,805).

As the additional corporation tax saving of £570 exceeds the employee's NI on the higher salary of £360, Susan is better off by paying a salary equal to the personal allowance rather than equal to the primary threshold. The impact of the employment allowance means that no employer NICs are payable where the salary is equal to the personal allowance.

If she pays a salary in excess of the personal allowance, the additional income tax payable, combined with employee NIC (totalling 32%), will outweigh any corporation tax deduction (at 19%), meaning it is better for the remainder of the employment allowance to remain unused.

Susan would have to pay over employee's NIC to HMRC.

71. Preserving The EA

The National Insurance employment allowance (EA) (set at £4,000 for 2020/21) is not available where the company only has one employee and that employee is also a director. This may be the case for a personal company with a single director and employee.

As noted at Tip 70, where the employment allowance is available, it can be beneficial to pay a salary equal the personal allowance (£12,500 for 2020/21). To ensure that the employment allowance remains available, a company must have more than one employee, or if the company only has one employee, that employee must not also be a director.

Personal companies where the sole employee is also the director who wish to retain entitlement to the employment allowance could consider employing another person, maybe a family member, or resigning as a director and appointing another person (perhaps a spouse or civil partner or other family member) as a director instead.

Preserving Entitlement to the EA

Hayley is setting up a personal company, H Ltd, and was intending to be the director and sole employee.

However, after speaking to her accountant as regards optimal profit extraction strategies, she decides not to be a director, appointing her husband as the director instead.

Although Hayley is the sole employee, as she is not also a director, she is able to claim the employment allowance. Consequently, it is beneficial for her to pay herself a salary equal to her personal allowance (set at £12,500 for 2020/21).

72. Optimal Salary For Under 21s

No employer's National Insurance is payable on an employee's (or director's) earnings where the employee is under the age of 21 until the employee's earnings exceed the employer's upper secondary threshold for under 21s, set at £962 per week for 2020/21. This means that where the director or employee is under 21 (for example, in a family company, maybe one or more of the director's children) the optimal salary for 2020/21 is equivalent to the personal allowance of £12,500 (assuming that this is not utilised elsewhere). It does not matter whether the employment allowance is available or not.

Note – care should be taken that the salary paid to the family member reflects the work done to preserve the corporation tax deduction.

Optimal Salary For Under 21s

The Brown family run their own family company; Brown Ltd. Mr Brown is the sole director. His wife and his daughter Charlotte, who is 19, are employed part-time by the company. He also employs a number of other employees and the employment allowance is fully utilised.

As his daughter Charlotte is under 21, it is beneficial to the family to pay her a salary of £12,500, as no employer's National Insurance is payable as her earnings are below the upper secondary threshold for under 21s (£50,000 per year for 2020/21).

73. Remuneration Or Dividend?

One of the perceived major benefits of incorporation is the ability to extract profits by way of dividends. The main advantage is the National Insurance saving, as no NICs are payable on dividends, whereas a salary payment would attract employee NICs of 12% or 2% and employer NICs of 13.8% (2020/21 figures) once the salary exceeds the primary and secondary thresholds.

In determining the optimal salary level for 2020/21, it is necessary to take account of the availability of the NIC employment allowance (for which see Tips 69 and 70).

All taxpayers receive a dividend 'allowance', regardless of their marginal rate of tax. This dividend allowance is set at £2,000 for 2020/21. However, this is not an 'allowance' as such, rather a zero-rate band which taxes the first £2,000 of taxable dividend income at a rate of 0%. Thereafter, dividends (which are treated as the top slice of taxable income) are taxed at 7.5% to the extent that they fall within the basic rate band, 32.5% to the extent that they fall with the higher rate band, and 38.1% to the extent that they fall within the additional rate band.

A payment of salary will attract tax at the taxpayer's marginal rate of income tax (20%, 40% or 45% (or for Scottish taxpayers at the relevant Scottish rate)). Salary payments are deductible in calculating profit for corporation tax purposes, unlike dividends which must be paid out of after-tax profits. Further, a dividend can only be paid if there are sufficient retained profits. In addition, various company law requirements must be met.

It is not simply a case that dividends are always best, although in many cases, taking dividends will result in less tax and National Insurance than taking a salary payment.

However, the best result will depend on the circumstances, as the decision whether to take salary or dividends will depend on the interaction of various factors – respective rates of income tax, corporation tax and National Insurance contributions, any other income that the taxpayer has and whether the company has sufficient retained profits.

To decide whether to extract profits by way of a dividend or a salary, crunch the numbers first. (The rates applying for 2020/21 and the financial year 2020 are used in the example.)

Salary Or Dividends – Crunching The Numbers

Paul is the director of a small company. He has profits of £20,000 (before corporation tax) and wants to know whether to extract them by way of a salary or a dividend. It is assumed that he has already received a small salary equal to his personal allowance.

He has a small number of employees and has utilised the NIC employment allowance in respect of employer's NIC payable in respect of earnings paid to his employees.

Via salary

Profits	£20,000
Less Employer's NIC	(£2,425)
Available to pay as salary	£17,575
Less Income Tax @ 20%	(£3,515)
Less NIC @ 12%	(£2,109)
Retained by shareholder	£11,951

There is no corporation tax to pay as taxable profits are reduced to nil after deducting salary of £17,575 and employer NIC of £2,425.

Via dividend

Profits   £20,000

Less Corporation Tax @ 19% (£3,800)

Distributed as a dividend   £16,200

Income Tax   (£1,065)

Retained by shareholder   £15,135

The whole dividend falls within the basic rate band (£37,500 for 2020/21). The first £2,000 of the dividend is taxed at 0% and the remaining £14,200 is taxed at 7.5%. The total tax payable on the dividend is therefore £1,065 ((£2,000 @ 0%) + (£14,200 @ 7.5%)).

In this situation, Paul is better off by paying a dividend as he is able to retain £15,135 of the profits, as compared to retaining only £11,951 if they are extracted by way of a salary payment.

74. Utilise The £2,000 Dividend Allowance

All individuals, regardless of the rate at which they pay income tax, are entitled to a dividend allowance. The dividend allowance is set at £2,000 for 2020/21.

The 'allowance' is not an allowance as such, rather a zero-rate band under which the first £2,000 of taxable dividend income is taxed at a rate of 0%. This allows all taxpayers, even those paying tax at the higher or additional rates, to receive £2,000 of dividend income in the tax year, tax-free.

This provides the opportunity to make a spouse or civil partner a shareholder in a personal or family company and take advantage of their dividend allowance to extract an additional £2,000 of post-tax profits, free of tax.

As dividend must be paid in proportion to shareholdings, using an alphabet share structure provides the flexibility to declare different dividends for different shareholders.

Utilise The £2,000 Dividend Allowance

Ann has her own company. She is married and her husband John is a marketing director with a salary of £80,000. Ann holds 100 ordinary shares and John holds 100 A ordinary shares.

By declaring a dividend of £2,000 for A ordinary shareholders, it is possible to utilise John's dividend allowance and extract profits from the company without any further income tax liability. Assuming Ann has already received dividends to utilise her allowance, paying £2,000 of dividends to John instead of further dividends to Ann will save tax at either 7.5% if Ann is a basic rate taxpayer (a saving of £150) or at 32.5% (a saving of £650) if Ann is a higher rate taxpayer.

The same approach can be adopted in relation to other family members to ensure that the benefit of their dividend allowance is not wasted and to enable more post-tax profits to be extracted free of further tax.

By having different categories of shares for each shareholder it is possible to overcome the restriction that shares must be paid in proportion to shareholding and tailor the dividends to the circumstances of the individual.

75. Extraction Or Accumulation?

Before deciding how to extract profits, it is first necessary to decide whether to extract profits or to retain them in the company.

Retaining profits will mean that they suffer only a corporation tax charge. Whereas, if profits are extracted, they may suffer income and, depending on how they are extracted, National Insurance contributions.

For the financial year that started on 1 April 2020, the rate of corporation tax is 19%. If no profits are extracted there will be no income tax to pay and no National Insurance, but the company will pay corporation tax at 19% on the profits. Retaining profits may be attractive if the funds are not needed outside the company, particularly if the shareholders have utilised their personal allowances elsewhere.

Accumulation may also be attractive if the shareholder has significant other income and any profits would be taxed at the higher or the additional rate.

However, if the shareholder has no other income it is likely profits will need to be extracted to cover living expenses. Extraction will also prevent the personal allowance being wasted and allow utilisation of the basic rate band. See tips 69 and 70 for the optimal salary depending on whether the EA is available. Profits extracted as a salary or bonus are deductible for corporation tax purposes, as is any employer's National Insurance contributions. Profits extracted in the form of pension payments (see Tip 83) are also deductible for corporation tax purposes.

As noted in Tip 73, once an optimal salary has been paid, it may be beneficial to extract further profits as dividends.

For 2020/21, the first £2,000 of taxable dividend income is taxed at a zero rate. To the extent that the personal allowance has not been fully utilised, dividends can also be extracted free of tax to use up any remaining personal allowance. So, if a salary has been paid equal to the primary threshold for 2020/21 of £9,500, it is possible to pay dividends of £5,000 (using the remaining personal allowance of £3,000 and the dividend allowance of £2,000) before any income tax is payable.

Beyond this level it may be preferable to leave funds in the company if they are not needed outside.

Extraction Or Accumulation?

Reginald is the sole director and shareholder of his one-man company.

In 2020/21, he has other income of £200,000. Although his company has made profits, Reginald is an additional rate taxpayer and does not wish to pay tax at the additional rate (45%) or the additional dividend rate (38.1%). As he has no other dividend income, he pays a dividend of £2,000 to utilise his dividend allowance for 2020/21 and receives the £2,000 of dividend income tax-free.

To avoid paying high tax rates, he retains the remaining profits within the company. His intention is to extract them in the future when he is able to do so at a lower marginal rate.

76. Use An Alphabet Share Structure

Where there are several shareholders, it is possible to minimise the total tax bill on extracted profits by first using each shareholder's personal allowance (if available), dividend allowance and then the remainder of their basic rate band, rather than paying all the dividends to one person and suffering tax on dividends at their dividend marginal rate.

However, unlike salary there is no flexibility to choose how much to pay each shareholder as dividends must be paid in relation to shareholdings. This restriction can be overcome by having different classes of shares for each shareholder so the dividend paid to each shareholder can be tailored each year.

This kind of share structure is often referred to as an 'alphabet' share structure as it is usual to designate different classes of shares by different letters of the alphabet, e.g. A ordinary shares, B ordinary shares, C ordinary shares, etc.

Note: Careful consideration should be given to the rights attaching to each class of share where the aim is to preserve future entitlement to business asset disposal relief (previously known as entrepreneurs' relief (see Tip 96)

Utilise An Alphabet Share Structure

DEF Ltd is a family company. Nick and his wife Rachel are shareholders and directors. Nick holds 100 A shares and Rachel holds 100 B shares.

In 2020/21, Nick has other income of £14,000 and Rachel has no other income. The personal allowance is set at £12,500 for 2020/21.

The company has post-tax profits of £60,000 they wish to extract as dividends.

As a starting point, it is possible to pay dividends of £2,000 to Nick tax-free to utilise his dividend allowance and to pay dividends of £14,500 to Rachel tax-free (to use both her personal allowance of £12,500 and her dividend allowance of £2,000). This leaves £43,500 to pay as dividends. Nick has £34,000 of his basic rate band remaining (£37,500 - £1,500 - £2,000) and Rachel has £35,500 of her basic rate band remaining (£37,500 - £2,000). As long as neither receives a dividend which is more than their remaining basic rate band, the remaining dividends will be taxed at 7.5% (a combined tax bill of £3,262.50 (£43,500 @ 7.5%).

Had all the profits of £60,000 been paid to Nick as a dividend, the associated tax bill would have been £10,350 ((£2,000 @ 0%) + (£34,000 @ 7.5%) + (£24,000 @ 32.5%)).

By having different classes of shares and paying dividends to both Nick and Rachel, their combined tax bill is reduced by £7,087.50

77. Timing Of Dividends

The timing of dividend payments can determine the tax payable. If the dividend allowance and basic rate band have already been utilised for one tax year, delaying the dividend until the start of the next tax year can save tax.

Likewise, if the personal allowance and dividend allowance for a year have yet to be fully used, accelerating the payment will allow any unused portion to be mopped up.

As a result of the impact of the Covid-19 pandemic, profits may be lower than usual in 2020/21. Where the business has retained profits, it may be viable to extract them in 2020/21 to use up allowances and lower rate tax bands that may otherwise be utilised.

Timing Of Dividends

Bob is the director and sole shareholder of his one-man company.

He is deciding whether to pay a dividend before the end of the 2020/21 tax year. In that year he has other income of £25,000. He has retained profits in the company of £100,000.

For 2020/21, the personal allowance is £12,500, the dividend allowance is £2,000 and the basic rate band is £37,500.

His other income of £25,000 uses up his personal allowance of £12,500 and £12,500 of his basic rate band, leaving £25,000 of his basic rate band available.

As he has not used his dividend allowance, the first £2,000 of any dividend paid is tax-free. This will use up £2,000 of his remaining basic rate band, leaving £23,000 available. If he needs to withdraw further funds from the company, he will pay tax at 7.5% on the next £23,000 of dividends paid (a total of £1,725). Thereafter, the dividend tax rate increases to 32.5% (costing him £325 in tax for each additional £1,000 of dividends paid). Once this level is reached, he may prefer to delay taking the money until a later tax year when his marginal rate of tax is lower.

Note: Once his income reaches £100,000 his personal allowance will start to abate. It is lost completely for 2020/21 where income exceeds £125,000.

78. Anticipated Profits

For a dividend to be payable the company must have sufficient retained profits to pay the dividend. If the company is loss making and there are no retained profits, the company cannot pay dividends. However, funds can still be extracted by means of a salary or bonus or extracted by other means (such as rent, pension contributions, etc.). Paying a salary or bonus will incur a NIC charge on the director if the amount paid exceeds the earnings threshold, and a NIC charge will fall on the company if the associated employer's NIC is not covered by the NIC employment allowance. Where the company anticipates making profits another option is for the director to have a loan from the company in anticipation of a future dividend, clearing the balance on the loan account by paying a dividend when the company is in profit.

However, a benefit in kind charge may arise in relation to the loan if the amount outstanding exceeds £10,000 at any point during the tax year. Further, if the loan account is still overdrawn nine months and one day after the end of the accounting period and the company is a close company (broadly one with five or fewer shareholders), corporation tax is payable on the outstanding balance of the loan at a rate of and of 32.5%.

Anticipated Profits

At 31 March 2020, M Ltd, a family company, has a negative balance sheet. The lack of retained profits means that it is not possible to pay a dividend.

Bill, the director, holds all the ordinary shares in the company. His wife and son hold A class shares.

During the following year, Bill takes out a director's loan of £30,000 to allow him to meet living expenses. The accounts for the year to 31 March 2021 are prepared in May 2021 and show a healthy profit.

The company declares a dividend of £40,000 in respect of the ordinary shares which is credited to Bill's loan account, clearing the overdrawn balance.

A benefit in kind tax charge is payable by the director on the benefit of the loan and the company must pay Class 1A NICs on the amount charged to tax.

By using the director's loan account rather than paying a salary it is possible to save tax and National Insurance, suffering only the benefits in kind charge on the loan and the associated Class 1A NICs.

The director will, however, have to pay tax on the dividend that is declared to clear the loan.

79. Bonus Or Salary?

Although paying a dividend rather than a salary will often be a more effective way of withdrawing profits, if the company is loss making and has no retained profits this will not be possible (but see Tip 78) and it may be necessary to pay a salary or a bonus to enable the director to meet his or her living costs.

Although from a tax perspective, it makes no difference whether a salary or bonus is paid, if the shareholder is not a director, paying a bonus can be the more efficient option as less employee National Insurance may be due.

However, if the employee is a director, there are no National Insurance savings to be had by paying a bonus rather than a higher salary, as directors have an annual earnings period for NIC and their NIC is recomputed on an annual basis at the end of the year.

Bonus Or Salary?

Grace is an employee in the family business but not a director. For 2020/21 she receives a salary of £792 per month to preserve entitlement to the state pension and contributory benefits. She is 30.

She wants to know whether it is better to receive additional salary of £2,000 a month (increasing her salary to £2,792 per month) or a bonus of £24,000 payable in December 2019.

It is assumed that the NIC employment allowance has already been utilised.

If she takes the additional salary she will pay additional employee National Insurance of £240 (12% of £2,000) per month (£2,880 a year) and the company will pay additional employer NIC of £276 (13.8% of £2,000) per month (£3,312 a year).

If she is paid a bonus of £24,000 in December 2020 (in addition to the regular monthly salary of £792) she will pay employee NIC on the bonus of £817.50 ((12% (£4,167 - £792) + 2% (24,792 – 4,167)) The company will pay additional employer NIC of £3,312 (£24,000 @ 13.8%).

Paying the bonus will reduce the employee NIC paid saving Grace £2,062.50 (£2,880 - £817.50).

This is because by paying a lump sum bonus rather than monthly payments of salary, much of the bonus attracts employee NIC at the additional rate of 2%, rather than the main rate of 12%.

The NIC paid by the employer is the same regardless of which route is taken.

80. Loss Making Companies

A company can only pay a dividend if there are sufficient retained profits from which to pay the dividend. There are no such restrictions on the payment of a salary.

Salary payments are deductible for corporation tax and there is no restriction on the payments where this creates or augments a loss.

In formulating an extraction policy in this situation, it is also necessary to take into account the way in which the loss is relieved. Carrying a loss back and setting it against profits of the previous year may generate a tax repayment, which may be valuable to the company.

Loss Making Companies

During the year to 31 March 2021, the company makes a profit of £10,000 before paying the director/shareholder. The company has a negative balance sheet. As there are no retained profits, it is not possible to pay a dividend as hoped so instead the company pays the director a bonus of £40,000 (on which employer NICs are £4,307.26 ((£40,000 - £8,788) @ 13.8%). The director had not drawn a salary and it assumed that the employment allowance has been used up elsewhere.

Taking account of the bonus and NIC turns the profit into a loss of £34,307.

If the company had sufficient profits in the preceding 12 months to utilise the loss, carrying the loss back would generate a tax repayment of £6,518.33 (19% of £34,307).

81. Employing Family Members

In a family company situation, it may be beneficial to employ family members, such as children or spouses, in order to extract profits from the company and to utilise unused personal allowances.

Care should be taken to ensure that the family member does some work in return for the income to avoid challenge from HMRC. Also, where the family member is not a director, they will need to be paid at least the National Living Wage (£8.72 per hour from 1 April 2020) if they are aged 25 and over or, if under the age of 25, the National Minimum Wage at the rate appropriate for their age.

The same principle can be extended to utilise basic and higher rate bands to reduce the overall family tax bill.

See also Tip 68 on paying a small salary to preserve state pension entitlement and also Tip 76 on having different classes of shares to pay different dividends to different shareholders. This can be beneficial to make use of each family member's tax-free dividend allowance, even if the person has income from other (non-dividend) sources.

Note: where family members or directors were furloughed during the Covid-19 pandemic, furlough grant payments need to be taken into account when computing the company's taxable profits. The grants paid to family members can be deducted, as can the associated employer's National Insurance.

Employing Family Members

Brown Ltd is a family company of which Ed Brown is the sole director and shareholder.

He is a higher rate taxpayer. He employs his wife Joanna and his three adult children Max, Zach and Emily, paying them each £12,500 to utilise their personal allowance for 2020/21.

No tax is due and but a small amount of employee's NIC will be due. No employer's NIC is due as the EA is available.

Ed is a higher rate taxpayer.

By paying his wife and children £12,500 each, which is received tax-free, rather than making an additional payment of £50,000 to himself, the family is able to save tax of £20,000 (£50,000 @ 40%) assuming that had the payments been made to Ed Brown instead in the form or additional salary or as a bonus, he would have paid tax on them at the higher rate of 40%. This strategy will also save National Insurance.

82. Beware The NLW And NMW Trap

Employees aged 25 and over must be paid at least the National Living Wage (NLW). This is set at £8.72 an hour from that date. Employees under the age of 25 must be paid at least the National Minimum Wage (NMW) for their age. From 1 April 2020, this is set at £8.20 an hour for workers aged 21 and over, £6.45 for workers aged 18 to 20, and at £4.55 an hour for workers under the age of 18 (but above compulsory school leaving age).

Dividends do not count towards the NLW or the NMW.

Potentially, the need to pay the NLW or NMW could be a problem if a shareholder/employee is paid a small salary and a dividend. However, a person can work up to 27 and a half hours a week and receive a salary equal to the personal allowance while being paid at the NLW.

However, the NLW/NMW does not apply to directors who do not have a contract of employment with the company, so appointing family members over the age of 16 as directors will overcome any NLW/NMW issues. Alternatively, family members can work on a part-time basis to ensure they remain within the NLW/NMW.

Note – To ensure compliance with NLW/NMW rules, family members who are employed by the company and who are not directors must be paid at least the NLW (or if under the age of 25, the NMW). This may impact on the profit extraction policy.

Beware The NMW Trap

Lucy is a shareholder and works for the family company. She is 26 and she is not a director. She works 15 hours a week. She must be paid at least £130.80 per week (NLW rate from 1 April 2020 of £8.72 per hour) to comply with NMW legislation.

Her brother Brad also works 15 hours per week. However, he is a director without a contract of employment so the NLW/NMW legislation does not apply.

83. Pay Pension Contributions

Paying contributions into a registered pension scheme can be an effective way of extracting profits from a family company.

Employer contributions can be made without limit, although they count towards the annual allowance. Contributions made in excess of the annual allowance attract a tax charge, although to the extent it is unused, the annual allowance can be carried forward up to three years.

The annual allowance is set at £40,000 for 2020/21. However, this is reduced by £1 for every £2 by which a person has adjusted net income in excess of £240,00 (income including pension contributions) where the person also has 'threshold income' (post-pension contribution income) of at least £200,000; subject to a maximum reduction of £36,000 (ensuring a minimum annual allowance of £4,000). The minimum annual allowance of £4,000 applies where income exceeds £312,000

Where a person has reached aged 55 and flexibly accessed a defined contribution plan, to prevent recycling of contributions, a reduced annual allowance, the Money Purchase Annual Allowance (MPAA) applies, set at £4,000 for 2019/20.

Note: employers must comply with the requirements of auto-enrolment. Directors without an employment contract are exempt from automatic employment.

Pay Pension Contributions

Bill and Louise are directors of their family company. They each have a registered pension scheme. Both have adjusted net incomes of less than £100,000.

In 2020/21 the company makes pension contributions of £20,000 each to their registered pension scheme. The £40,000 paid by the company is deductible for corporation tax purposes.

84. Tax-Free Benefits And Expenses

The tax legislation provides exemptions from tax (and National Insurance) for certain benefits in kind.

Making use of the exemptions offers a further opportunity to extract funds from a family company without triggering a tax or NIC charge.

Popular exemptions include mobile phones, childcare and childcare vouchers. Providing the benefit rather than the funds with which to buy the benefit saves tax. The costs are also deductible in computing the company's profits.

Note: Following the introduction of the alternative valuation rules from April 2017, the ability to use salary sacrifice arrangements to tax advantage of tax exemptions has been seriously curtailed.

Tax-Free Benefits And Expenses

Ravi and Helen are directors of their family company. Their children, Jack and Palie, also work for the company.

The company takes out a contract for four mobile phones and provides each member of the family with a mobile phone. The bills are paid by the company and are deductible in computing profits.

The family members receive the use of a phone tax-free. They do not need to fund one from their post-tax income.

85. Pay Interest On Account Balances

If a director has a credit balance on his or her loan account, opportunities exist for paying interest on the balance.

If the personal savings allowance (£1,000 for basic rate taxpayers or £500 for higher rate taxpayers for 2020/21) is available, no tax will be payable on the interest in the hands of the director. No NIC is payable either. This makes it preferable to paying a salary.

To keep HMRC happy, the interest should be at a commercial rate and not excessive.

The interest paid is deductible in computing the company's profits as long as it is actually paid to the director (rather than merely credited to the director's account) within 12 months of the end of the accounting period. The company should deduct tax at the basic rate of 20% from the interest and pay it over to HMRC on a quarterly basis.

However, in the current climate of low interest rates, the options for extracting profits in the form of interest are limited.

Pay Interest On Account Balances

Derek has lent money to his family company to fund expansion and his director's account has a credit balance of £50,000. He is a higher rate taxpayer.

The company pays interest at a rate of 1% per annum. The interest received by Derek of £500 must be included on his self-assessment return, but it is the personal savings allowance (set at £500 for higher rate taxpayers). It is paid to him net of basic rate tax of 20%, but as no tax is due he can reclaim the tax deducted from HMRC.

The company enjoys a corporation tax deduction for the interest paid. It must return details of the tax deducted to HMRC on form CT61 on a quarterly basis and pay the tax deducted over to HMRC.

86. Making Loans To Directors

Funds can be made available by a loan. Although there are tax consequences of making loans, it is possible for the director to have the use of the money for up to 21 months for a minimal cost. The rules also apply where a director's current account is overdrawn.

Under the close company rules for loans to participators, a corporation tax charge arises on the outstanding loan balance if the loan has not been repaid nine months and one day after the year end (the normal corporation tax due date). The charge is 32.5% of the loan balance (equal to the higher rate of dividend tax). This is known as a 'section 455' charge.

An income tax charge will also arise under the benefit in kind legislation if the director has loans outstanding at any point in the tax year with a balance of £10,000 or more if the loan is interest-free or if the interest paid on the loan is less than that payable at the official rate (set at 2.25% from 6 April 2020 and at 2.50% for 2019/20). If the loan is repaid by the corporation tax due date, there is no section 455 tax to pay. The benefit in kind charge, should one arise, will be cheaper than paying interest on a commercial loan. In this way, a loan from the company can be a cheap source of funds.

It should be noted that anti-avoidance provisions apply to prevent the loan being repaid to avoid the tax charge and the funds subsequently being re-borrowed within a 30-day period or where there is an intention to re-borrow the funds at the time the repayment is made (even if this is outside the 30-day period). However, the anti-avoidance provisions do not apply to repayments and reborrowing of less than £5,000, providing limited planning opportunities to reduce the tax payable.

Making Loans To Directors

Ivan is a director of a family company. The company prepares accounts to 30 November.

On 1 December 2018 Ivan borrowed £40,000 from the company. This is at the start of the accounting period to 30 November 2019.

The loan is repaid on 25 August 2020, which is within nine months of the accounting period end. Consequently, there is no tax to pay on the loan balance.

However, Ivan must pay a benefit in kind charge on the loan. This spans three tax years.

The loan is outstanding for 126 days in 2018/19 and the official rate of interest is 2.50%. The cash equivalent of the benefit is £345 (£40,000 x 2.50% x 126/365).

Assuming that Ivan is a higher rate taxpayer, he will pay tax on the benefit of the loan of £138. The company will pay Class 1A NIC of £47.61.

The loan is outstanding for all of 2019/20. Assuming, the official rate of interest is 2.50%, the cash equivalent of the benefit is £1,000 (£40,000 @ 2.50%), costing Ivan £400 in tax and the company £138 in Class 1A NIC.

In 2020/21, the loan is outstanding for 142 days. The official rate of interest is 2.25%, the cash equivalent of the benefit is £350 (£40,000 @ 2.25% x 142/365).

The associated tax payable by Ivan is £140 and the Class 1A NIC payable by the company is £48.30.

Ivan has the use of £40,000 for almost 21 months for a total cost of £912 (tax of £678 and Class 1A NIC of £234).

This is equivalent to an interest rate of 1.3% – considerably less than if he had taken out a commercial loan.

87. Small Loans To Directors

As illustrated in Tip 85, making a loan to a director can be advantageous.

Under the benefit in kind rules, no tax charge arises in respect of an employment-related loan if the balance outstanding on the loan does not exceed £10,000 at any point during the tax year.

This means that it is possible for a director to enjoy a tax-free loan of up to £10,000 for up to 21 months free of charge.

Beware of the temptation to repay the loan and immediately reborrow the money as HMRC may issue a challenge as anti-avoidance provisions render repayments of more than £5,000 ineffective if the funds are re-borrowed within 30 days.

www.taxinsider.co.uk   Chapter 6

88. Loans Written Off

Beware of the special rules that apply where a loan to a participator in a close company is written off. Most family companies are close companies and the rules will bite when writing off an overdrawn balance on a director's loan account.

For income tax purposes, the amount written off is treated as a distribution (like a dividend). If the dividend allowance is available, the first £2,000 of the taxable dividend is tax-free (being taxed at the zero rate). Thereafter, it is taxed at, respectively, 7.5%, 32.5% and 38.1% to the extent that it falls within the basic, higher and additional rate bands.

However, unlike a dividend, NIC is payable on a loan written off. This will cost the director 12% or 2% depending on whether his or her income exceeds the upper earnings limit and will cost the company 13.8%.

A further sting is that there is no corporation tax deduction for the loan written off.

Depending on the tax and NIC position of the director, rather than writing the loan off, it may be preferable to leave it outstanding as, once the NIC charge is taken into account, it may be cheaper to pay the corporation tax charge on the outstanding loan, particularly as this is recovered if the loan is eventually repaid.

Where the loan is written off in the capacity of a shareholder rather than as an employee, strictly speaking NIC should not be due. However, this is a tricky area and professional advice should be sought.

155

Loans Written Off

Jenny has a loan of £20,000 from her family company, in which she is director and shareholder. The loan was taken out in 2019. The company is considering writing off the loan.

It is assumed that the National Insurance employment allowance is not available to set against any employer's National Insurance that may arise.

If the loan is written off in 2020/21, she will be treated as receiving a dividend of £20,000. If it is assumed that she has received a salary equal to her personal allowance, but has no other income, the first £2,000 of the dividend is tax-free as it is covered by her dividend allowance.

The remaining £18,000 is taxed at 7.5%, generating a tax bill of £1,350 (£18,000 @ 7.5%). She will also pay NIC @ 12% on the amount written off (£2,400, being 12% of £20,000). The company will pay NIC of £2,760 (13.8% of £20,000). The tax and NIC cost of the write off is therefore £6,510.

However, if she has a salary of £50,000 and is a higher rate taxpayer, she will still receive the first £2,000 of the dividend tax-free (as it is covered by her dividend allowance), but the remaining £18,000 is taxed at the dividend higher rate of 32.5%, generating a tax bill £5,850.

She will also pay National Insurance of £400 (£20,000 @ 2%) and the company will pay NIC of £2,760 (£20,000 @ 13.8%).

The total tax and NIC cost of the write off is £9,010. If the loan is left outstanding, the company must pay corporation tax of 32.5%

on the normal corporation tax due date. This will cost the company £6,500, which is cheaper than the cost of writing off the loan.

Further, if any part of the loan is repaid, the associated s. 455 tax can be recovered.

89. Extract Profits In the Form of Rent

Where the business is based at home or at another property owned by the director personally, it is possible to extract profits in the form of rent paid for the use of the home office or other premises.

Although the rent is taxable in the hands of the director, there is no NIC to pay. Further, the company can deduct the rent in computing its taxable profits for corporation tax purposes.

If the director/shareholder has losses from other property rentals, paying rent will enable those losses to be mopped up. This is because losses from a property rental business can only be offset against profits from that business.

Where rent is paid by a company to a director, it is advisable to draw up a rental agreement between the director and the company.

Extract Profits In The Form Of Rent

David is a director and shareholder in his family company, which is run from his home. The company pays him rent of £400 per month for the use of the home office.

David also has two properties which he rents out. In the tax year in question he makes a loss on those properties of £5,000.

The rent from the family company is taken into account in computing the profits or losses of the property rental business and the rent of £4,800 received from the company is offset against the loss of £5,000 from the other properties to give a net loss of £200.

As the rent paid to David by the company is offset by other property losses, David pays no tax on it and is able to utilise the property income losses from his other properties.

The company enjoys a corporation tax deduction of £4,800 in respect of the rent paid to David, saving corporation tax of 19%.

Chapter 7.
Employing People

90. Pay PAYE On Time

91. Beware The Salary Sacrifice Trap

92. File RTI Returns On Time To Avoid Penalties

90. Pay PAYE On Time

Penalties are charged if PAYE is paid late on more than one occasion in the tax year. The penalty is a percentage of the tax paid late. The percentage depends on the number of occasions in the tax year when payment has been made late.

Systems should be put in place to ensure payment reaches HMRC on time. Where payment is made electronically, cleared funds must reach HMRC's account by 22nd of the month. If payment is made by cheque, the cheque should reach HMRC by 19th of the month. Where the due date falls on a non-banking day (Saturday, Sunday or bank holiday), payment should reach HMRC by the last banking day before the due date.

Late payment penalties are charged in-year on a quarterly basis.

Interest is also charged on payments made late. It is charged in-year after the outstanding amount has been paid.

91. Beware The Salary Sacrifice Trap

The opportunity to use salary sacrifice arrangements to take advantage of tax exemptions has been significantly. From 6 April 2017, alternative valuation rules apply to most benefits when they are made available under an optional remuneration arrangement (OpRA), such as a salary sacrifice or flexible benefits arrangement, or one where a cash alternative to the benefit is offered instead. Under the alternative valuation rules, the benefit is valued for tax purposes at the higher of the salary foregone or the cash alternative offered and the amount computed under the normal cash equivalent rules. Where the rules apply, the benefit of the tax exemption is lost.

However, salary sacrifice arrangements remain beneficial for the benefits to which the alternative valuation rules do not apply. These are:

- employer-provided pension savings;

- employer-provided pension advice;

- childcare vouchers;

- employer-supported childcare;

- workplace nurseries;

- employer-provided cycles and cyclists' safety equipment (including 'cycle to work' schemes; and

- low-emission cars with CO_2 emissions of 75g/km or less.

Instead, the benefit is valued using the normal cash equivalent rules (which for exempt benefits is zero). For low emission cars, the benefit is valued using the company car rules.

Under a salary sacrifice arrangement, the employee gives up cash salary which is liable to tax and employee and employer NIC in return for an exempt benefit. The employee saves tax and NIC and the employer saves employer NIC. By swapping cash salary for an exempt benefit to which the alternative valuation rules do not apply, it is possible to save tax and employer and employee NIC.

It should be noted that the tax exemptions for childcare vouchers and employer-supported childcare are only available where the employee joined the employer's scheme prior to 4 October 2018.

Beware The Salary Sacrifice Trap

Jake employs several people in his business. He operates a salary sacrifice scheme to allow employees to take advantage of tax exemptions.

Katie joined her employer's childcare voucher scheme prior to 4 October 2018. She takes advantage of the salary sacrifice scheme. She is a basic rate taxpayer and swaps £2,860 of cash salary for childcare vouchers of £55 per week. The vouchers are exempt from tax and NIC.

She saves tax of £572 and NIC of £343.20, so is £915.20 a year better off. The company saves employer NIC of £394.68. Everyone wins.

However, if Katie had swapped £600 for an employer provided mobile phone, under the alternative valuation rules, the benefit of the mobile phone would be valued at £600 (the foregone salary). The benefit of the associated exemption would be lost. Katie would be taxed on a benefit worth £600 and her employer would also pay Class 1A NIC.

Salary sacrifice arrangements are now only beneficial for a handful of exempt benefits.

92. File RTI Returns On Time To Avoid Penalties

Under real time information (RTI) employers are required to provide details of pay and deductions to HMRC electronically (via a full payment submission (FPS)) on or before the time at which payment is made to the employee. Where no payments are made in the tax month, HMRC must be advised of this by means of an employer payment summary (EPS).

Penalties apply to RTI reports filed late. A penalty will be charged where an FPS is not received as expected and HMRC have not received an EPS to indicate that no FPS was due. No penalty is charged for the first month in which returns are made late. Thereafter a fixed monthly penalty applies, which depends on the number of employees in the PAYE scheme. The penalties will be levied in-year on a quarterly basis.

HMRC allow a three-day period of grace before a penalty is charged. However, this is a concession not a three-day extension to the filing period and it should not be relied on. HMRC may penalise employers who routinely file within this three-day window.

Chapter 8.
Using Losses

1. Loss Relief Options For The Self-Employed

2. Carry Back A Trading Loss For Corporation Tax Purposes

93. Loss Relief Options For The Self Employed

If you make a loss in your trade, profession or vocation there are various ways in which that loss can be relieved. It is important to consider all the options to ensure that best use is made of the loss. This may be particularly relevant for businesses that suffered losses as a result of the Covid-19 pandemic.

The general rule is to obtain relief for tax at the highest rate of tax possible (as this will generate the biggest repayment) and as early as possible.

The options are to set the loss against:

- other income for the tax year in which the loss is made;

- capital gains of the same year;

- total income and gains of the previous tax year; or

- future profits of the same trade.

Special rules apply to losses in the early years of a trade (see Tip 28) and to losses on cessation (see Tip 100).

As it is not possible to tailor how much of the loss is used, if the loss exceeds income for the year of the claim, your personal allowance will be lost. Seeking to preserve personal allowances should form part of the loss relieving strategy.

Loss relief must be claimed. It should also be noted that certain income tax reliefs, including loss reliefs, are capped at the greater of £50,000 and 25% of income. This may impact on the optimal loss relieving strategy.

Loss Relief Options For The Self-Employed

Elliot is self-employed and has been in business for many years. In the year to 30 April 2020 (tax year 2020/21) he makes a loss of £20,000.

He has other income of £15,000 in 2020/21 and capital gains of £7,000.

In 2019/20 he had income of £40,000.

The best course of action is for him to set the loss against his income of 2019/20 as this will generate a tax repayment of £4,000 (£20,000 @ 20%).

If he sets the loss against other income of 2020/21, he will lose the benefit of his personal allowance. Similarly, there is no point extending the claim to capital gains as these are covered by his annual exemption (set at £12,300 for 2020/21).

The best result is obtained by carrying the loss back.

94. Carry Back A Trading Loss For Corporation Tax Purposes

As with individuals (see Tip 93) companies should take care to use any losses that they make effectively. This may be particularly relevant where a company suffers a loss a result of the Covid-19 pandemic.

Where a company makes a trading loss, the loss can be relieved by carrying it back and setting it against the profits of the preceding 12 months as long as the company was carrying on the same trade in accounting periods that fall in the preceding 12 months. If the previous period was profitable, carrying the loss back will generally be the preferred option as it will generate a corporation tax repayment. For companies struggling with cash flow difficulties, this can provide a welcome cash injection.

If the loss cannot be utilised by carrying it back, it can be carried forward and set against future trading profits.

Special rules apply to terminal losses (see Tip 100).

If the company is a member of a group, the loss can be surrendered to other group companies.

Carry Back A Trading Loss For Corporation Tax Purposes

UVW Ltd suffers a loss of trade during the Covid-19 pandemic and makes a trading loss of £40,000 in the year to 31 March 2021. In the year to 31 March 2020, it made a trading profit of £35,000.

The company makes a claim to carry back £35,000 of the loss to the year ended 31 March 2020.

This generates a corporation tax repayment of £6,650 (£35,000 @ 19%) (plus interest). The balance of the loss (£5,000) is carried forward for set-off against future profits.

Chapter 9.
The End Of The Business

1. Plan Your Exit Strategy

2. Claim Business Asset Disposal Relief

3. Spouses, Civil Partners and Business Asset Disposal Relief

4. Gift Hold-Over Relief

5. Overlap Relief

6. Terminal Loss Relief

7. Post-Cessation Receipts And Expenses

8. BONUS TIP: Reclaiming VAT After You De-Register

95. Plan Your Exit Strategy

No one can work forever and there will come a time when you want to pass on, sell or wind up your business, hopefully to be able to enjoy the fruits of your labour.

To achieve the best possible outcome, it is advisable to plan your exit strategy at least a couple of years in advance. Some people find it useful to set a planned retirement date and use this as a deadline to work towards. Planning considerations will include:

- whether you wish to retain any on-going involvement, for example in a consultancy or advisory role;

- whether you need to groom a successor;

- whether you wish to pass on the business to family members;

- whether you wish to withdraw capital from the business and how it will be funded;

- whether you wish to sell any shares;

- how ownership of the business will be shared in the future;

- how transfers of shares or assets can be arranged in a tax efficient manner;

- if selling the business, whether you are selling shares or assets;

- how the best price can be obtained; and

- how the consideration should be structured.

It is essential that professional advice is obtained well in advance to achieve the best possible result.

96. Claim Business Asset Disposal Relief

Business asset disposal relief (previously known as entrepreneurs' relief) provides relief against capital gains tax on qualifying gains made by an individual on the disposal of all or part of the business, the assets in the business after it has stopped trading and shares in a personal trading company. HMRC Helpsheet 275 has more details on the relief.

Gains that qualify for entrepreneurs' relief are taxed at 10% up to the maximum lifetime limit. The lifetime limit is set at £1 million for qualifying disposal on or after 11 March 2020. Prior to this date, the lifetime limit was been £10m.

For those with gains income and gains in excess of the basic rate limit, this relief is very valuable and can save tax of up to £100,000 (£1 million @ 10%).

However, its availability is contingent on certain conditions being met. The conditions must be met throughout the qualifying period.

This is the period ending on the date the asset was sold or business ceased, if earlier, set at two years for qualifying disposals that take place on or after 6 April 2019.

Where shares are sold the qualifying period is two years ending on the date that the shares are sold, the date that company ceases to be a member of a trading group, or the date on which it stops trading.

The conditions depend on the type of disposal. If you dispose of all or part of your business, you must either own it directly or be a partner in the partnership that owns it.

If you dispose of assets following cessation, you must own the business directly or be a partner in the partnership that owns it. The assets must be disposed of within three years of the date on which the business ceases.

If the disposal is of shares or securities in your personal company, you must hold at least 5% of the ordinary share capital and that holding must give you 5% of voting rights in the company.

You must also be entitled to 5% of the company's distributable profits and 5% of its assets available for distribution to equity holders in a winding up or meet the alternative test of 5% of the sale proceeds if the company is sold. You must also be an employee or officer of the company or of a company in the same trading group.

The condition must also be met throughout the qualifying period, set at two years for disposals made on or after 6 April 2019.

When planning an exit strategy action should be taken to ensure that the qualifying conditions are met throughout the applicable qualifying period. Planning ahead is essential.

Claim Entrepreneurs' Relief

John has operated as a sole trader for many years and wishes to retire. He has planned ahead for the disposal making sure that he has met the conditions necessary to qualify for business asset disposal relief. The business ceases on 31 May 2020 and he disposes of assets used in the business on 28 August 2020, realising a gain of £60,000.

He has other gains in the year which utilise his annual exemption and is a higher rate taxpayer.

He meets the conditions for business asset disposal relief. The gain is taxed at 10% generating a capital gains tax bill of £6,000.

Had he not met the conditions for the relief, he would have had to pay capital gains tax of £12,000 on the gain (£60,000 @ 20%).

Claiming business asset disposal relief saves tax of £6,000 (£60,000 @ 10%).

97. Spouses, Civil Partners and Business Asset Disposal Relief

Spouses and civil partners are entitled to their lifetime limit of £1 million for business asset disposal relief, potentially doubling the tax savings on offer.

Both spouses or civil partners must meet the qualifying conditions. In relation to the disposal of shares in a personal company, this means that each person must hold at least 5% of the ordinary share capital with at least 5% of voting rights and be entitled to at least 5% of the distributable assets and 5% of the assets available to equity holders throughout the two years, ending with the date on which the shares are sold or the date on which the company ceases to trade. Where the company is sold, the alternative test of entitlement to 5% of the proceeds may be met instead.

The individual must also be an employee or officer of the company or of a company in the same trading group.

Shares can be transferred between spouses and civil partners on a no-gain no-loss basis. Transferring shares two years before the planned disposal date will ensure both parties meet the conditions and maximise relief. Shares can also be transferred to pass the gain from one party to another to maximise relief.

Husband And Wife And Entrepreneurs' Relief

Owen and Rita are husband and wife and are shareholders in the family company. Owen owns 97% of the shares and voting rights. The remaining 3% are owned by Rita. The company has been very successful. They plan to retire and expect to realise a gain of £2m on the sale of their shares.

Their accountant advises Owen to transfer 47% of his shareholding to Rita (so they each own 50% of the shares) on a no-gain no-loss basis and to wait at least at least two years before selling the shares. They take this advice and 30 months later sell the shares, each realising a gain of £1m.

They claim business asset disposal relief and each pay capital gains tax of £100,000 (it is assumed their annual exemption is utilised elsewhere and they have not previously used any of their lifetime limit). Their total combined capital gains tax bill is £200,000. They both meet the employment condition.

Had they not transferred the shares, Owen would have realised a gain of £1.94m. As the gain is more than the lifetime limit of £1m for disposal on or after 11 March 2020, he would only be entitled to business asset disposal relief in respect of £1m of the gains; the remaining £940,000 would not qualify for the relief.

Consequently, he would pay capital gains tax of £288,000 ((£1m @ 10%) + (£940,000 @ 20%)).

Rita would make a gain of £60,000 and as she would not meet the qualifying conditions for business asset disposal relief she would pay capital gains tax of £12,000 (assuming she too is a higher rate taxpayer). Their combined bill would be £300,000 (£288,000+ £12,000).

Forward planning and transferring shares to Rita has saved them £100,000.

98. Gift Hold-Over Relief

Business assets may be given to other members of the family. In this situation gift hold-over relief may be claimed. This allows the gain to be 'held over' so that the tax on it is deferred until the recipient sells the asset.

This generates cash-flow advantages.

Gift Hold-Over Relief

Nigel has been a sole trader for many years operating in business as a mechanic. He wants to retire and pass the business to his son, so gives him his workshop.

He originally bought the workshop for £20,000 and at the date he gives it to his son it has a market value of £60,000. He makes a gain of £40,000.

The gain is held over. When his son sells the asset, his cost is the market value of £60,000 less the held-over gain of £40,000, i.e. £20,000.

The tax is deferred and there is nothing to pay by Nigel when making the gift of the workshop to his son.

99. Overlap Relief

In the opening years of an unincorporated business some profits may be taxed twice because of the way the basis period rules work in the opening years (see Tip 22).

Relief for overlap profits is given in the final year of assessment. Overlap profits are deducted in working out the profits for the final tax year.

The deduction of overlap profits can create or increase a loss.

Overlap Relief

Ian has been in business for many years preparing accounts to 31 October each year.

He wants to retire and his business ceases on 31 May 2020. The profits for the period 1 November 2019 to 31 May 2020 are £70,000 and are assessed in 2020/21.

He has overlap profits of £25,000.

Relief is given for overlap profits by deducting them from the profit for the final tax year (i.e. £70,000 for seven months to 31 May 2020). The profits for 2020/21 are reduced to £45,000 as a result of the availability of overlap relief.

100. Terminal Loss Relief

Special rules apply to terminal losses. This relief may be particularly relevant to individuals and companies whose businesses cease trading as a result of the Covid-19 pandemic and may generate valuable tax repayments.

Individuals

A person may decide to stop trading if they are making losses. Special rules apply to relieve terminal losses.

A claim for terminal loss relief can be made if the person permanently ceases to carry on a trade and makes a terminal loss. The terminal loss is the loss made in the period beginning at the start of the final tax year and ending with the date of cessation, plus any loss from the period starting with the date 12 months prior to the date of cessation and ending on 5 April prior to cessation. The terminal loss may be relieved against the profits of the trade for the final tax year and previous three tax years. Relief is given against a later year before an earlier year.

Alternatively, the loss can be set against total income (and extended to capital gains) of the year of the loss and/or the preceding year.

Terminal Loss Relief: Individuals

Barry is self-employed and has been in business for a number of years. He prepares accounts to 31 March each year. His trade ceases on 30 June 2020.

He makes a profit of £10,000 for the year to 31 March 2020 and a loss of £16,000 for the period from 1 April 2020 to 30 June 2020. He has overlap profits of £5,000 to relieve.

His terminal loss is £13,500 ((9/12 x £10,000) - £16,000 - £5,000).

He makes profits of £9,000 for the year to 31 March 2019 (taxed in 2018/19) and £25,000 for the year to 31 March 2018 (taxed in 2017/10).

He claims terminal loss relief.

The profits for 2019/20 have been taken into account in computing the terminal loss.

The loss is set first against 2018/19 (£9,000) with the remaining £4,500 being set against the profits of 2017/18.

Companies

Terminal loss relief is also available for the loss made by a company in its final accounting period. The loss can be carried back and set against profits of the previous three accounting periods. Relief is given against the most recent year first.

The relief must be claimed.

Terminal Loss Relief: Companies

DEF Ltd prepares accounts to 31 August each year. It ceases trading on 31 August 2020 and makes a loss for that year of £75,000.

It made a profit of £30,000 for the year to 31 August 2019, a profit of £35,000 for the year to 31 August 2018, and a profit of £50,000 for the year to 31 August 2017.

Terminal loss relief is claimed.

£30,000 of the loss is carried back and set against the profits of the year to 31 August 2019.

£35,000 of the loss is carried back and set against the profits of the year to 31 August 2018.

The remaining £10,000 is carried back and set against the profits for the year to 31 August 2017.

Carrying the loss back generates repayments of corporation tax plus interest.

101.Post-Cessation Receipts And Expenses

Income tax is charged on post-cessation receipts arising from a trade, profession or vocation to the extent it is not otherwise charged to tax. A post-cessation receipt is a receipt that a person receives after a trade has been permanently discontinued which arises from the carrying on of the trade before cessation.

In computing the amount that is charged to tax, a deduction is given for losses and expenses or debits that would have been deductible had the trade continued. No deduction is given for amounts arising directly or indirectly from the cessation itself.

Post-Cessation Receipts And Expenses

After the cessation of the trade, John receives a payment of £5,000 in respect of an unpaid invoice arising from the trade which has been written off as a bad debt.

He incurred costs of £500 in recovering the debt.

He is taxed on £4,500, being the amount of the receipt less the cost of recovery.

102. BONUS TIP: Reclaiming VAT After You De-Register

A VAT-registered business will need to de-register on cessation. After de-registration there are some limited circumstances in which input tax can be reclaimed. This may be valuable where a business has ceased trading as a result of the impact of the Covid-19 pandemic.

VAT can be reclaimed in respect of goods and services supplied prior to de-registration. VAT on debts that go bad after the registration is cancelled can also be recovered as long as the associated output VAT was paid over to HMRC prior to de-registration. Again, this may be pertinent where debtors' businesses fail as a result of the Covid-19 pandemic.

Claims should be made on form VAT 427 and sent to HMRC as soon as possible after de-registration.